The Northwest Happenings Guide

Oregon Edition July 2015 – June 2016
By: Catherine Pittman

Your Guide to Bazaars, Fairs, Festivals, Parades,
Carnivals, Craft Shows, Farmers Markets Fireworks and
Other Oregon Events & Attractions

A Product of the Northwest Happenings Guide
A Subsidiary of Pitter Patter Productions
Tualatin, Oregon

Distributed by

The Northwest Happenings Guide
A Subsidiary of Pitter Patter Productions

Visit Us Online!

www.pitterpatterproductions.com
www.NWhappeningsguide.com

Dedication

To Seeking Fun in Our Own Backyard,
Letting Our Inner Child Free,
Discovering Our Artistic Muse
And Living Life to Its Fullest!

Cover Design By:
Catherine Pittman

Cover Images Used With Permission

Top Left: Oktoberfest © Oaks Park Association
Top Center: Oregon Coast Historical Railway
Christmas Lights, Coos Bay, OR
© Victoria Ditkovsky
Top Right: Multnomah Falls © Brigitte Werner
Center Right: Pioneer Log Fortress Defense Tower
Ft. Vancouver, WA © Capricornis
Center Image: Oregon State Shape Mount Hood
Design by: Catherine Pittman
Mount Hood Image by: TPSDave
Center Left: Harney County Royalty
© Harney County Fair Association
Lower Left: Seattle Skyline Fireworks – Alki Park
© Nilanjan Bhattacharya
Lower Left 2: Mountain Biking © Jacek Chabraszewski
Lower Center Left Group:
  Top Left: Playful Sea Otter © Peng Ge
  Top Right: Festa Italiana
© Festa Italiana Association
  Lower Left: Oregon Coast © Bill Kuffrey
  Lower Right: Whale Watching Image © Jorge Felix
Lower Right
Corner: Happy Boy Riding Horse
© Crazy80frog

The Northwest Happenings Guide

2015 Oregon or Washington Editions
July 2015 - June 2016

Who is the guide for?
- Families seeking kid-friendly events & attractions
- Artisans and Crafters seeking exhibit space
- Food vendors seeking vendor space
- Promotors seeking visitors & vendors
- Visitors to the Northwest seeking local, fun attractions

What type of events are in the guide?
- Bazaars
- Carnivals
- Fairs - County, State, Street & Neighborhood Fairs
- Festivals
- Farmers Markets
- Local Year-Round Attractions & Amusement Parks
- Baby & Kid Shows
- Bridal Shows
- Home Remodel & RV Shows
- Halloween Mazes, Pumpkin Farms & Haunted Houses
- Christmas Events
- Fireworks

How do I get my own copy?
Available in two formats: Paper and Kindle Ebook on
Amazon.com or www.nwhappeningsguide.com. Paper
version also available on CreateSpace.com

The Northwest Happenings Guide
A Subsidiary of Pitter Patter Productions
Tualatin, Oregon
www.NWhappeningsguide.com www.pitterpatterproductions.com

Bazaars

Craft Shows

Food Vendors

Arts & Crafts

Music Festivals

Holiday Fun

Fairs

Farmers Markets

Carnivals

Halloween Mazes & Fright Towns

Artisan Marketplaces

County Fairs

Petting Zoos

Wine & Beer Tasting

Fireworks

Festivals

Parades

Street Festivals

Neighborhood Fairs

Began in March thru 2015

3/1/2015 - 12/24/2015
Portland Saturday Market 2015
Downtown Portland - Portland, OR
www.portlandsaturdaymarket.com   (503) 222-6072

Portland's beloved market is celebrating its 42nd season this year! This ithe Rose City's largest outdoor arts and craft market for Northwet artisans to show off their skills and sell their handmade items.   Market includes live music, exotic foods, and plenty of handmade arts and crafts!

Free Admission
Hours: Sat: 10am - 5pm; Sun: 11am - 4:30pm

Vendor Contact: reid@saturdaymarket.org
# of Vendors: 350   # of Years Held: 42

3/7/2015 - 11/7/2015
Weekend Guided Tours at Leach Botanical Garden
6704 SE 122nd Ave. - Portland, OR
www.leachgarden.org   (503) 823-1671

No registration required. Meet in front of Manor House, first-come, first-served: maximum tour size 15 visitors. Join Gardener/Curator on the first Saturday of each month for a seasonal exploration of the garden. Other Saturdays join a volunteer guide for an informative guided tour of the garden with weekly themes.

Free Admission
No Kid's Activities
Hours: Every Saturday 2015, 11:00am-noon
(March through October, & first Saturday in November)

3/21/2015 - 11/1/2015
Oregon Caves Park
On Hwy 46 at 201 - Cave Junction, OR
www.nps.gov

Guided Tours. Discover the Oregon Caves and learn about geology, fossils, old-growth forest, cave ife, bats and more. Get off the beaten path and learn about caving techniques, etiquette and conservation. Caving is a great sport for those who enjoy physical an dmental challenges in their quest to experience fun, new places! We also have Candlelight Cave Tours during the summer. Fridays and Saturdays only, 6:30 pm, ages 12 & up.

Admission: Not Provided

4/6/2015 - 11/14/2015
Eugene Saturday Market
126 E 8th - Eugene, OR
www.eugenesaturdaymarket.org   (541) 686-8885

Eugene's Saturday Market is a weekly celebration of local arts, food and music. Over 250 artisans sell their handcrafted goods, seventeen food booths serve up an international array of foods, and the stage features six different live music acts each day. In operation since 1970, the Market is the oldest weekly open-air crafts festival in the U.S. Open every Saturday, rain or shine, April through mid-November in a beautiful park setting.

Free Admission
Kid Friendly Event
Hours: Saturday only, 10am - 5pm

Vendor Contact: Vi Sadhana
visadhana@eugenesaturdaymarket.org
# of Vendors: 250   Juried Event
Attendance: 2,000-5,000 weekly
# of Years Held: 46

4/9/2015 - 10/31/2015
Lithia Artisans Market
Calle Guanajuato Lithia Park - Ashland, OR
www.lithiaartisansmarket.com   (888) 303-2826

This Ashland tradition showcases the best local music and the finest artisans of the region!

Free Admission
Hours: Saturdays: 10am - 6pm; Sundays: 11am - 5pm

Attendance: 2000   # of Years Held: 32

5/1/2015 - 9/30/2015
Family Nature Discovery Days
32275 Fox Hollow Rd - Eugene, OR
www.eraptors.org   (541) 485-1320

Held the last Sunday of the month, May through September from noon - 4pm. Visit the raptors and participate in themed activities. Activity fee is waived for those hiking the Ridgeline Trail or arriving via bike. These for discovery days: 5/31/15 - Birds in Springtime - Paint an egg and make a nest; 6/28/15: The Art of Nature - Make an art desing using the nature that surrounds us, suc as rocks, leaves, shells, seed pods, etc.; 7/26/15: Wildlife Play Hospital - Rescue an "injured" stuffed animal and help it get better; 8/30/15: All About Owls - Owl pellet dissection and make a pine cone owl; 9/27/15: Migration Station 0 Mouse hunt activity.

Paid Attraction
Kid Friendly Event
Hours: Last Sunday, May - September, noon - 4pm

Vendor Contact: info@eraptors.org

5/6/2015 - 10/21/2015
Coos Bay Wednesday Farmers Market
Hwy 101 & Central Ave - Coos Bay, OR
www.coosbaydowntown.org   (541) 269-0215

This open-air market features farm fresh produce, baked goods, plants and more!

Free Admission
Hours: Wednesdays Only 9am - 3pm

5/10/2015 - 10/11/2015
Astoria Sunday Market
167 W Grand - Astoria, OR
www.astoriasundaymarket.com   (503) 325-1010

Farm produce, local arts and crafts, food, music and more bring to life the downtown street market.

Free Admission
Hours: Sundays Only: 10am - 3pm

# of Years Held: 15

5/30/2015 - 10/31/2015
Saturday Farmers Market
9th St & Klamath Ave - Klamath Falls, OR
www.klamathfallsfarmersmarket.org
(541) 273-1102

Farm product, artisans, music, kids activities and more each Saturday until 10/31/15

Free Admission
Kid Friendly Event
Hours: Saturdays Only: 9am-1:30 pm

Attendance: 900

6/1/2015 - 6/1/2016
Double Mountain Horse Ranch
Year Round Trail Rides & Kids' Camps - Hood River, OR
www.ridinginhoodriver.com   (541) 513-1152

Double Mountain Horse Ranch will guide you on your own adventure through the breathtaking Columbia River Gorge. Ride for a couple of hours or make it a day; we have the right horse and itinerary for every age and ability. Tour the orchards, wineries or secret fishing spots with majestic Mt Hood and Mt Adams on the horizon. Plan the perfect party or event, stage your senior or family portraits. Your adventure awaits!

Free Admission
Kid Friendly Event
Hours: M-Sun 8 am - 7 pm

Vendor Contact: Margo Goodman
horseandhair@embarqmail.com

6/6/2015 - 9/27/2015
Gold Rush Bandits Train Robberies
McEwen Depot - Baker City, OR
www.sumptervaleyrailroad.org

The whole family will enjoy the Gold Rush Bandit Train Robbberies! This historic shooting group employs period firearms and costumes for their horseback mounted robbcrics. Fun for all ages! 2015 robery dates are: 6/6, 7, 27, 28; 7/18 and 19, 8/1,2,15,16,29 & 30; 9/12,13,26 & 27

Paid Admission
Kid Friendly Event

Vendor Contact: info@sumptervalleyrailroad.org

6/6/2015 - 11/21/2015
Saturday Outdoor Growers' Market
Downtown 4th St & F St - Grants Pass, OR
www.growersmarket.org   (541) 816-1144

Featuring the finest fresh fruits & vegetables growing in Sourthern Oregon, as well as artisans with their handcrafted wares, gourmet specialty foods.

Free Admission
Hours: Saturdays: 9am - 1pm

6/11/2015 - 9/10/2015
Wilsonville Farmers Market
Sofia Park - 28836 Costa Circle W - Wilsonville, OR
www.wilsonvillemarket.com

Free Admission
Hours: Thursday Evenings, 4pm - 8pm

6/13/2015 - 9/26/2015
Tualatin Farmers Market
Tualatin Public Library Parking Lot - Tualatin, OR
www.tualatinfarmersmarket.com

Quality produce, meat and dairy products, hot food & drinks, local consumer goods.

Free Admission
Hours: Saturdays, 8:30 am - 12:30 pm

Vendor Contact:
market@tualatinfarmersmarket.com

6/15/2015 - 8/21/2015
Oregon Zoo Summer Day Camps
4001 SW Canyon Rd - Portland, OR
www.oregonzoo.org   (503) 226-1561

Children 4 years old thru 8th grade explore the habits
and daily lives of some of the zoo's residents!

Paid Admission
Kid Friendly Event

Vendor Contact: info@oregonzoo.org

6/15/2015 - 9/28/2015
Portland Farmers Market at the Square
Pioneer Courthouse Square - Downtown - Portland, OR
www.portlandfarmersmarket.org   (503) 241-0032

Free Admission
Hours: Monday's: 10am - 2pm

# of Vendors: 30

---

*A perfect summer day is when the sun is shining, the breeze is
blowing, the birds are singing, and the lawn mower is broken.
~~James Dent, American Author & Sportswriter*

*In summertime the crickets play their tiny strings,
A sweet little song begins!
A Hoot owl calls from an old oak tree,
"Little cricket, I will add the harmony!"
Together their voices fill the night until dawns first light!
Hear a tree frog croaking in a meadow glen,
"Little owl and cricket may I please join in?"
Together they all sing, out your window their song rings,
Carried gently by the sweet summer wind.
~~© Catherine Pittman 2015 Inspired by "A Summer Lullaby"
from the album, The Dream Faerie*

July 2015

7/1/2015 - 8/31/2015
Noon Tunes Summer Concert Series
Pioneer Courthouse Square - Downtown - Portland, OR

This summer concert series features music from some of Portland's best regional and local musical talent! Sponsored by 101.9 Kink. There is a total of 8 concerts, and includes food vendors making the Square a downtown destination for your summer lunch time!

Free Admission
Hours: Tuesdays: 12pm - 1pm

7/1/2015 - 7/4/2015
St. Paul Rodeo & Wild West Art Show
Rodeo Grounds - St. Paul, OR
www.stpaulrodeo.com   (503) 989-3369

This rough and tumble 4th of July celebration will bring fun to your family's holiday celebration. Featuring one of the top rodeos of the nation, youth rodeo, trail ride, carnival and western art show.

Admission: Not Provided
Kid Friendly Event

Vendor Contact: Jennifer Crosby
spr.showcase@gmail.com
Juried Event
Attendance: 50000   # of Years Held: 79

7/1/2015 - 9/6/2015
Summer Concerts at the Zoo
4001 SW Canyon Rd - Portland, OR
www.oregonzoo.org   (503) 226-1561

Bruce Horsby, Indigo Girls, John Butler Trio, and more! Check website for dates & concerts.

Paid Admission
No Kid's Activities

Vendor Contact: info@oregonzoo.org

7/2/2015 - 8/6/2015
Albany River Rhythms Concert Series
Monteith Riverpark - Albany, OR
www.riverrhythms.org   (541) 917-7771

Kids art area fun is open 5:30-7pm. Featuring gourmet food, blanket area seating at our stage on a first-come, first-served basis. Concerts are held on the following dates: 7/2/15, 7/9/15, 7/23/15, 7/30/15 and 8/6/15.

Free Admission
Kid Friendly Event
Hours: Begins at 5:30 pm

Vendor Contact: Lynne Smith
Lynne.smith@cityofalbany.net   Deadline: 4/6/15

A painter paints pictures on canvas. But musicians paint their pictures on silence. ~~ Leopold Stokowski, Brittish Conductor 1882 – 1977

There is nothing in the world so much like prayer as music is. ~~William P Merrill, American Presbyterian Clergyman 1867- 1954

Music is what life sounds like.~~Eric Olson, Author

7/2/2015 - 7/4/2015
La Pine Frontier Days
La Pine Event Center - La Pine, OR
www.lapinefrontierdays.org   (541) 536-7821

The fund includes a parade, jamboree, fun lawnmower races, home brew contest, talent show, kid's carnival, artisan booths and a midway stage filled with the great sounds of music!

Admission: Not Provided
Kid Friendly Event
Hours: 10am - 10pm

Vendor Contact: Ann Gawith
info@lapinefrontierdays.org
Deadline: 6/25/15   # of Vendors: 100
Attendance: 4000   # of Years Held: 28

7/2/2015 - 7/5/2015
Western Days 2015
Riverview Park - Independence, OR
www.westerndays.net

Carnival rides, artisans, entertainments, and children's activities with a magnificent fireworks display over the river on both days. Admission is just $1 for everyone over the age of 6.

Paid Admission
Kid Friendly Event
Hours: Thurs: 12pm12am; Fri: 12pm-10pm; Sat: 12pm-12am. Fireworks begin at 10pm for both the July 3rd & July 4th shows

Vendor Contact: vendorinfo@westerndays.net
Deadline: 6/20/15   # of Vendors: 40
Attendance: 30000   # of Years Held: 31

7/3/2015 - 7/5/2015
Art and the Vineyard Festival with Freedom
Festival Fireworks
Alton Baker Park, 100 Day Island Rd - Eugene, OR
www.artandthevineyard.org   (541) 345-1571

The 2015 Art and the Vineyard Festival with July 4th
Freedom Festival Fireworks takes place July 3rd, 4th,
and 5th in Alton Baker Park, Eugene, Oregon. An annual
July 4th weekend family event, the festival features over
80 artists in the Artists' Marketplace, an Art For Your
Garden area, a Wine Court with 27 Oregon vineyards, an
International Food Court, a Youth Art Arena, Youth
Stage, and a Main Stage, with entertainment throughout
the weekend.

Paid Admission
Kid Friendly Event
Hours: Fri, 11am - 9:30pm; Sa. 11am through the
Fireworks; Sun. 11am - 6:30pm

Vendor Contact: Karen Marie Pavelec, Executive
Director, Maude Kerns Art Center
staff@mkartcenter.org
Deadline: 3/27/15
# of Vendors: 100 plus   Juried Event
Attendance: 20000   # of Years Held: 31

Bluegrass has brought more people together and made more
friends than any music in the world. You meet people at
festivals and renew acquaintances year after year.
~~ Bill Monroe, Musician

7/3/2015 - 7/4/2015
Estacada Timber Festival
Estacada Timber Park - Estacada, OR
www.estacadatimberfestival.com   (800) 630-7858

The Estacada Timber Festival is back with a 2 day event. Friday night July 3rd will start off at 5pm with live music and dancing. On Saturday July 4th 11am Gates open for Timber games such as log rolling, pole climbing, bucking, sawing, log stacking, and horse log pulls will be joined by lots of fun activities for the kids as well as food, drinks, and vendors. Saturday night ends with a big bang with one of Clackamas Counties largest firework shows! visit www.EstacadaTimberFestival.com for more information.

Paid Admission
Kid Friendly Event
Hours: Friday 5pm -11pm Saturday 11am-11pm

Vendor Contact: Jordan Winthrop
vendor@estacada4thofjuly.com
Deadline: 6/15/15   # of Vendors: 30
Not a Juried Event

Festivals are fun for kids, fun for parents and offer a welcome break from the stresses of the nuclear family.
The sheer quantities of people make life easier: Loads of adults for the adults to talk to, and loads of kids for the kids to play with.
~~ Tom Hodgkinson, Author

I entreat all artisans faithfully to follow their craft and take delight in it.
~~ Jan Hus, Cezechoslovakian Philosopher 1369 - 1415

7/3/2015 - 7/5/2015
Eugene Gem Faire
Lane County Events Center - Eugene, OR
www.gemfaire.com   (503) 252-8300

Fine jewelry, precious & semi-precious gemstones, millions of beads, crystals, gold & silver, minerals & much more at manufacturer's prices. Over 70 exhibitors from around the world. Jewelry repair & cleaning while you shop. Free hourly door prizes. For more info, visit www.gemfaire.com or call (503) 252-8300 or email: info@gemfaire.com.

Paid Admission
No Kid's Activities
Hours: Fri Noon-6pm,
         Sat 10am-6pm,
         Sun 10am-5pm

Vendor Contact: Allen Van Volkinburgh
info@gemfaire.com
Deadline: until full
# of Vendors: 70   Not a Juried Event
Attendance: 4000   # of Years Held: 26

7/3/2015 - 7/3/2015
Fireworks in the Garden
Oregon Garden - Silverton, OR
www.oregongarden.org
(877) 674-2733 or (503) 874-8100

Admission: Not Provided
Kid Friendly Event

Vendor Contact: info@oregongarden.org

7/3/2015 - 7/3/2015
July 3rd Fireworks
The Oregon Garden - Silverton, OR
www.oregongarden.org/events/july-3rd-
fireworks/   (503) 874-8100

Join us on July 3rd for Silverton Day, great food and
drink, live music and a beautiful fireworks display,
planned by the Oregon Garden Foundation & presented
by Roth's™ Fresh Markets. Live music by The FlexTones
will start at 7pm in Founder's™ Square, in the Silverton
Market Garden.   After 6pm, admission is free for
everyone for the fireworks. A donation of $5 per family is
suggested to help cover the cost of the fireworks.

Free Admission
Kid Friendly Event
Hours: 6pm - 11:30pm

Vendor Contact: Mary Ridderbusch-Shearer
info@oregongarden.org
Deadline: April
# of Vendors: varies   Not a Juried Event
Attendance: 2000
# of Years Held: 15

7/4/2015 - 7/4/2015
Ashland 4th of July Celebration
Downtown & Community Center - Ashland, OR
www.ashlandchamber.com   (541) 482-3486

Free Admission
Kid Friendly Event

A man's country is not a certain area of land, of mountains,
rivers and woods, but it is a principle; and patriotism is loyalty
to that principle.
~~ George William Curtis, American Writer, 1824 - 1892

7/4/2015 - 7/4/2015
Ashland Old Fashioned 4th of July
Winburn Way in Lithia Park - Ashland, OR
www.ashlandchamber.om
(541) 482-3486, ext. 104

This great "small town's" festivities begins early with a run, followed by a grand old parade, activities for the entire family, food and entertainment in the gorgeous setting of Lithia Park. The fun day concludes with spectacular fireworks.

Free Admission
Kid Friendly Event

Vendor Contact: Kelsey Holderness
kelsey@ashlandchamber.com
# of Vendors: 100   Attendance: 15000

7/4/2015 - 7/4/2015
Boardman Thunder 4th of July Celebration
Marina Park - Boardman, OR
www.boardmanchamber.org   (541) 481-3014

Event includes a 5/10K Fun Run and Walk, parade, games, and fireworks. Fun for the entire family!

Free Admission
Kid Friendly Event
Hours: 8am - 10pm

Vendor Contact: info@boardmanchamber.org
# of Vendors: 15   Attendance: 2000
# of Years Held: 31

If our country is worth dying for in time of war, let us resolve that it is truly worth living for in time of peace.
~~ Hamilton Fish, United States Secretary of State 1808 - 1893

7/4/2015 - 7/4/2015
Gleneden Beach 4th of July Parade & Craft Fair
Eden Hall - Gleneden Beach, OR
www.glendenbeach.org   (541) 764-3203

Celebrate the 4th at Gleneden beach with this day filled
with fun events! Featuring a pancake breakfast, parade,
craft fair and food booths.

Free Admission
Kid Friendly Event
Hours: 10am - 4pm

Vendor Deadline: 6/7/15

7/4/2015 - 7/4/2015
North Plains 4th of July "A Wild West" Celebration
Downtown - North Plains, OR
www.np4july.org   (503) 647-5555

Free Admission
Kid Friendly Event
Hours: 7am - 10pm

Vendor Contact: info@northplains.org
Attendance: 4000

My early childhood memories center around this typical
American country store and life in a small American town,
including 4th of July celebrations marked by fireworks and
patriotic music played from a pavilion bandstand.
~~Frederick Reines, American Physicist 1918 – 1998

PANCAKE BREAKFAST   CAR SHOW   GOOD FOOD   AWARDS   PARADE   FAMILY FUN

LIVE MUSIC   PIE EATING CONTEST   VENDORS   WILD WEST EVENTS   FIREWORKS

19th Century
Activities,
Challenges &
Competitions

NORTH PLAINS
FOURTH of JULY

A Day-Long
Family Friendly
Celebration of
Wild West Events

FOURTH OF JULY

A WILD WEST CELEBRATION
9AM-10:30PM
Patriotic Events Families & Friends
Information at www.np4july.org

FRIENDS
NORTH PLAINS PUBLIC LIBRARY

Columbia
Bank

KNIGHTS OF PYTHIAS
FRIENDSHIP CHARITY BENEVOLENCE

7/4/2015 - 7/4/2015
Old Fashioned July 4th Celebration
Drake Park - Bend, OR
www.bendparksandrec.org   (541) 706-6134

A Bend tradition since the 1930's, over 10,000 people come from all over Oregon and beyond! Featuring a pet parade that preceeds the festival, then join the festivities at Drake Park for live music, games, shopping at over 100 artisan and community booths, and plenth of food!

Free Admission
Kid Friendly Event
Hours: 11am - 4pm

Vendor Contact: Charlene Schulz
char@bendparksandrec.org
# of Vendors: 110   Attendance: 10000

7/4/2015 - 7/4/2015
Rockaway Beach July 4th Celebration
Ocean's Edge Wayside - Rockaway Beach, OR
www.rockawaybeach.net

One of the largest celebrations on the North Coast, beginning with the Independence Parade at 11am. The day's festivities include a bake sale, dachschund races, a flyover by the National Guard and the day ending with spectacular fireworks at around 10pm.

Admission: Not Provided
Kid Friendly Event

Vendor Contact: rbccsec@gmail.com

7/6/2015 - 7/8/2015
Clay Studio for Ages 10-15
Spark Arts Center, 1805 NE Cesar Chavez Blvd, Portland,
OR 97212 - Portland, OR
www.sparkartscenter.com   (503) 281-6757

During this 2 day workshop you will learn hand building
techniques to design, build, and glaze sculptures of your
choice.

Paid Admission
Kid Friendly Event
Hours: Monday, July 6, 1-3pm and Wednesday, July 8,
1-3pm

7/6/2015 - 8/3/2015
Concerts in the Park - Sellwood Neighborhood
Sellwood Riverfront Park - SE Spokane & Oaks Pkwy
Portland, OR

Free Admission
Hours: Mondays - 6:30 pm

7/7/2015 - 7/21/2015
Concerts in the Park - Columbia
Columbia Park Annex - N Woolsey & Willamette Blvd -
Portland, OR

Free Admission
Hours: Tuesdays - 6:30 pm

7/7/2015 - 7/28/2015
Concerts in the Park - Mt Tabor
Mt Tabor Park - SE 69th & Taylor - Portland, OR

Free Admission
Hours: Tuesdays - 6:30 pm

7/8/2015 - 7/29/2015
Concerts in the Park - Dawson
Dawson Park - Portland, OR

Free Admission
Hours: Wednesdays - 6:30 pm

7/8/2015 - 7/29/2015
Concerts in the Park - Willamette
Willamette Park - Portland, OR

Free Admission
Hours: Wednesdays - 6:30 pm

7/9/2015 - 7/9/2015
American Music Festival
Azalea Park - Brookings, OR
www.brookings.or.us   (541) 469-3181

Food and beverages are available for sale. Bring your
blanket or lawn chair and remember... no alcohol is
allowed. If it rains, the concert is moved to the VFW Hall
at 206 Pacific Ave.

Free Admission
Hours: 1pm

7/9/2015 - 7/23/2015
Concerts in the Park - Glenhaven
Glenhaven Park - Portland, OR

Free Admission
Hours: Thursdays - 6:30 pm

*When an American says that he loves his country, he means not
only that he loves the New England hills, the prairies glistening
in the sun, the wide and rising plains, the great mountains and
the sea. He means that he loves an inner air, an inner light in
which freedom lives and in which a man can draw the breath of
self-respect.*
~~ Adlai Stevenson II, American Statesman, 1900 – 1965

7/9/2015 - 7/12/2015
Marion County Fair
State Fairgrounds - Salem, OR
www.co.marion.or.us/cs/fair/   (503) 585-9998

Something for everyone in the entire family! Plenty of contests, animals, kid activities, and food.

Paid Admission
Kid Friendly Event

Vendor Contact: Denise Clark
declark@co.marion.or.us
# of Vendors: 60   Attendance: 25,000
# of Years Held: 33

7/9/2015 - 8/27/2015
Movies in the Garden
The Oregon Garden - Silverton, OR
www.oregongarden.org/events/movies-in-the-garden/   503-874-8100

Join us for a movie outdoors every Thursday evening, July 9th - August 27th, 2015 Doors will open at 7pm, and the show will begin at dusk on the beautiful Garden Green, in the heart of The Oregon Garden. It's also a great opportunity to catch a sunset in the Garden! Parking will be available in the lower parking lot, across from the Pavilion. Please, no outside food or drink. Food will be available for purchase.

Paid Admission
Kid Friendly Event
Hours: 7pm - 11:30pm

Vendor Contact: Mary Ridderbusch-Shearer
info@oregongarden.org
Deadline: April   # of Vendors: varies
Not a Juried Event
Attendance: 50-150/event   # of Years Held: 4

7/9/2015 - 8/13/2015
Munch & Music Series in Drake Park
Drake Park - Bend, OR
www.c3events.com   (541) 383-3026

Celebrating our 25th anniversary this year, the Munch & Music is a free concert series and one of Bend's summertime favorites! Held each Thursday, the weekly series provides great music, arts and outstanding food.

Free Admission
Kid Friendly Event

Vendor Contact: artists@c3events.com
Deadline: 7/1/15   # of Years Held: 25

7/10/2015 - 9/30/2015
Art in the Garden
Oregon Garden - Silverton, OR
www.oregongarden.org
(877) 674-2733 or (503) 874-8100

Admission: Not Provided
Kid Friendly Event

Vendor Contact: info@oregongarden.org

To fans in a festival setting it's like a picnic. You want to have a good time with your friends in that crowd. And in the background you hear the band play, 'Oh that's my favorite song!' everone is there to enjoy the afternoon.
~~Tom Araya, Musician

This nation wil remain the land of the free only so long as it is the home of the brave.
~~Elmer Davis, Reporter & Peabody Recipient 1890-1958

7/10/2015 - 7/12/2015
Bend Summer Festival
Downtown Bend - Bend, OR
www.c3events.com   (541) 383-3026

Festival features fine artists and craftspeople, artisans and performers with five stages of some of the best regional and national blues, rock and jazz.

Paid Admission
Hours: Fri: 5pm-10pm;
        Sat: 11am-10pm;
        Sun: 11am-5pm

Vendor Contact: artists@c3events.com
Deadline: 6/25/15   Juried Event
Attendance: 75000+   # of Years Held: 24

7/10/2015 - 7/31/2015
Concerts in the Park - Fernhill
Fernhill Park - Portland, OR

Free Admission
Hours: Fridays - 6:30 pm

7/10/2015 - 7/12/2015
Lincoln County Fair
Lincoln County Fairgrounds - Newport, OR
www.townandcountryfair.com   (541) 351-1160

Paid Admission
Kid Friendly Event
Hours: Fri/Sat: 10am-9pm; Sun: 10am-6pm

Vendor Contact: Debra Jones
newportdebbie@peoplepc.com
# of Vendors: 48
Attendance: 7000   # of Years Held: 107

7/10/2015 - 7/12/2015
Oregon Country Fair
Route 126 - Veneta, OR
www.oregoncountryfair.org   (541) 343-4298

Filled with world-class entertainment, handcrafted works of art, delectable food, educational displays and magical surprises at every turn!   It's an experience that is unequal in the festival world!

Admission: Not Provided
Hours: 11am - 7pm

Vendor Contact: office@oregoncountryfair.org
Deadline: 4/1/15   # of Vendors: 350
Juried Event
Attendance: 45000   # of Years Held: 46

7/10/2015 - 7/12/2015
Portland Bead Faire
Oregon Convention Center - Portland, OR
www.gemfaire.com   (503) 252-8300

Millions of beads from around the world, including Czech, glass, lampwork, gold, silver, gemstone, crystal, pearl, and one of a kind at manufacturer's prices. Over 70 importers, exporters and wholesalers from around the world will be on site. Jewelry repair while you shop. For more info, call (503) 252-8300 or email: info@gemfaire.com. Visit www.gemfaire.com.

Paid Admission
No Kid's Activities
Hours: Fri Noon-6pm, Sat 10am-6pm, Sun 10am-5pm

Vendor Contact: Allen Van Volkinburgh
info@gemfaire.com
Deadline: until full   # of Vendors: 70
Not a Juried Event
Attendance: 4000   # of Years Held: 26

7/10/2015 - 7/12/2015
Portland Holiday Gem Faire
Oregon Convention Center - Portland, OR
www.gemfaire.com   (503) 252-8300

Paid Admission
No Kid's Activities
Hours: Fri: 12pm-6pm;
        Sat: 10am-6pm;
        Sun: 10am-5pm

Vendor Contact: info@gemfaire.com
Deadline: 5/25/15   # of Vendors: 100

7/10/2015 - 7/12/2015
Portland Vintage Racing Festival
Portland International Raceway - Portland, OR
www.SVRA.com   (503) 665-3483

This festival is one the oldest and longest-running vintage races in the United States, drawing 250 or more competitors from West Coast and Canada.

Spectators have full access to paddock area, providing the opportunity to take in this rolling history of motorsports up close and personal, as well as talking to drivers and crewmembers. Saturday night's party starts as the checkered flag waves over the last race group, music by Mitch Ryder & the Detroit Wheels, and a fireworks display.

Portland International Raceway is a 12-turn, 1.9-mile circuit built on the Vanport site, a town completely destroyed by a flood in 1948.

Paid Admission   Hours: 8am-5pm

Vendor Contact: Sandy Bauer twobauers@msn.com
Deadline: 7/1/15   # of Vendors: 40
Attendance: 15,000

7/10/2015 - 7/11/2015
Sisters Artist Marketplace
Downtown - Sisters, OR
www.centraloregonshows.com   (541) 420-0279

Admission: Not Provided

Vendor Contact: Richard Esterman
centraloregonshows@gmail.com
Juried Event   Attendance: 10000
# of Years Held: 3

7/10/2015 - 7/11/2015
Turkey Rama
3rd St / Downtown - McMinnville, OR
www.mcminnville.org/about-mcminnville-area-
chamber-of-commerce/turkeyrama/

Free Admission
Hours: 10am - 9pm

Vendor Contact: Holly Goodman
hgoodman@mcminnville.org

7/11/2015 - 7/11/2015
Chalk Art Contest
Lincoln City Cultural Center - Lincoln City, OR
www.lincolncity-culturalcenter.org/events/chalk-
art-contest   (541) 994-9994

Paid Admission
Kid Friendly Event

...And I'm proud to be an American,
Where at least I know I'm Free.
And I won't forget the men who died,
Who gve that right to me.
~~Lee Greenwood, Musician & Songwriter

7/11/2015 - 7/11/2015
Kids Obstacle Challenge
Lee Farms - Tualatin, OR
www.kidsobstaclechallenge.com

All participating kids will receive a custom dated military dog tag award to commemorate their accomplishments on the obstical course, plus goodies our sponsor have to offer! Prents are free to run alongside their children.

Paid Admission
Kid Friendly Event
Hours: 10am - 1pm; Check-in Opens at 9:30 am

Vendor Contact: eight18productions@gmail.com

7/11/2015 - 7/11/2015
Mississippi Street Fair
N Mississippi Ave between Fremont & Skidmore
Portland, OR
www.mississippiave.com/streetfair

The Mississippi Street Fair is Portland's largest street fair. Come see over 40 bands on 5 stages with a Kids Zone, Dunk Tank, Vendors, Beer Gardens, great restaurants, Grandfather's rib-off, performers, and fun for all.

Free Admission
Kid Friendly Event
Hours: Open 10:00 am - 9:00 pm

Vendor Contact: Brad Nelson
streetfair@mississippiave.com

Deadline: None	# of Vendors: 250
Not a Juried Event	Attendance: 25,000+
# of Years Held: 14	

7/11/2015 - 7/12/2015
Sandy Mountain Fest
Meining Memorial Park - Sandy, OR
www.sandymountainfestival.org   (503) 668-5900

Every July we celebrate artists and music at Sandy's Meinig Memorial Park! Over 150 artisans show and sell their wares, while live entertainment is provided on two stages. Come enjoy mouthwatering treats from over 20 food booths manned by the local non-profit organizations.

Admission: Not Provided
Hours: Sat: 10am - 8pm; Sun: 10am-6pm

Vendor Contact: smfa@sandymountainfestival.org
# of Vendors: 150   Juried Event
Attendance: 5000   # of Years Held: 43

7/11/2015 - 7/11/2015
WAAAM Traffic Jam - A Car
Show and Swap Meet
1600 Air Museum Road
Hood River, OR
www.waaamuseum.org   541-308-1600

Vehicles (all types including cars, motorcycles, trucks, etc.) must be 30+ years old for show entry. On Friday registered participants and their guests "cruise the gut" and end the day with food and a drive-in movie. Saturday is the Swap Meet and Car Show with judging and prizes for entrants and drawings for visitors. WAAAM is located three miles from downtown Hood River at 1600 Air Museum Road, Hood River, OR 97031.

Paid Admission
Kid Friendly Event   # of Years Held: 4
Hours: Daily 9am-5pm Event Hours 8am-5pm

7/15/2015 - 7/19/2015
Columbia County Fair
Columbia County Fairgrounds - St. Helens, OR
www.columbiacountyfairgrounds.com
(920) 992-5691

Talent show, carnival, exhibits, live entertainment, rodeo and more!

Paid Admission
Kid Friendly Event
Hours: Wed & Thur: 10am - 10pm;
        Fri & Sat: 10am - 12am;
        Sun: 10am-5pm

Vendor Contact:
info@columbiacountyfairgrounds.com
# of Vendors: 90   Attendance: 30000
# of Years Held: 164

7/15/2015 - 7/18/2015
Crooked River Roundup Horse Races
Crook County Fairgrounds - Prineville, OR
www.crookedriverroundup.com   (541) 447-4479

Offering a variety of exciting events and family-friendly activities that are bound to be a hootin' hollering good time! Plenty of activities, contests, and a bonanza of food and gift vendors.

Paid Admission
Kid Friendly Event

# of Vendors: 10   Attendance: 8000
# of Years Held: 70

7/15/2015 - 7/18/2015
Linn County Fair
Linn Co Fairgrounds - Albany, OR
www.linncountyfair.com   (541) 926-4314

Four days of animals, live entertainment, carnival rides, delicious food and fun for your family!

Paid Admission
Kid Friendly Event

Vendor Contact: Randy Porter rporter@co.linn.or.us
# of Vendors: 115   Attendance: 25000

7/15/2015 - 7/19/2015
Oregon High Desert Classic I
62895 Hamby Rd - Bend, OR
www.oregonhighdesertclassics.org (541) 389-1409

Admission: Not Provided

Vendor Contact: Zoe Gilbert zgilbert@jbarj.org

7/16/2015 - 7/20/2015
Seadog Nights & Gypsy Carnival
Cheadle Lake Park - Lebanon, OR
www.seadognights.com

Admission: Not Provided
Kid Friendly Event

I question not if thrushes sing,
If roses load the air;
Beyond my heart I need not Reach,
When all is summer there.
~~John Vance Cheney, American Poet 1848 - 1922

7/17/2015 - 7/19/2015
Miners Jubilee
Geiser Pollman Park - Baker City, OR
www.minersjubilee.com   (541) 525-3673

Admission: Not Provided
Kid Friendly Event

Vendor Contact: jjvela@bakercityherald.com
Deadline: 5/1/15

7/17/2015 - 7/18/2015
Oregon Berry Festival
Ecotrust Event Spaces - Portland, OR
www.oregonberryfestival.com   (503) 505-3876

Come all ye berry lovers! You know it's summer in
Oregon when the ripest, juciest berries start appearing
in decadent pies, james and treats! Come celebrate
everything berry! Fresh berry vendors with berry
products galore, cooking demos, kids booth with berry
themed crafts, and a Gala Berry Dinner prepared by one
of Portland's finest chefs!

Admission: Not Provided
Kid Friendly Event
Hours: Fri: 12pm - 6pm; Sat: 11am - 5pm

Attendance: 5000

7/17/2015 - 7/19/2015
Oregon International Airshow
Hillsboro Airport - Hillsboro, OR
www.oregonairshow.com   (503) 629-0706

Paid Admission
Kid Friendly Event
Hours: Fri: 6pm-9pm; Sat & Sun: 9am-5pm

Vendor Contact: info@oregonairshow.com
Attendance: 70000   # of Years Held: 28

7/17/2015 - 7/19/2015
Robin Hood Festival of Sherwood
Old Town Sherwood - Sherwood, OR
www.robinhoodfestival.org   (503) 625-4233

Free Admission
Kid Friendly Event
Hours: Fri: 5pm-11pm;
           Sat: 11am-11pm

Vendor Contact: robinhoodfestival@gmail.com
Deadline: 7/1/15
# of Vendors: 110   Juried Event
Attendance: 15000   # of Years Held: 64

7/17/2015 - 7/19/2015
Salem Art Fair & Festival
Bush's Pasture Park - Salem, OR
www.salemart.org   (503) 581-2228

Held in picturesque Bush's Pasture Park, this family-
friendly event features an art fair with over 200 regional,
national and international artists, two entertainment
stages, craft beer and wine gardens, food courts, kids'
court and more!

Admission: Not Provided
Kid Friendly Event

Vendor Contact: Debbie Leahy debbie@salemart.org
Deadline: 2/2/15
# of Vendors: 200   Juried Event
Attendance: 50000   # of Years Held: 41

---

*...To lie sometimes on the grass under the trees on a summer's
day, listening to the murmur of water, or watching the clouds
float across the blue sky, is by no means waste of time.*
~~John Lubbock, "Recreation," The Use of Life, 1894

7/18/2015 - 7/19/2015
Deschutes Dash Weekend Sports
Riverbend Park - Bend, OR
www.deschutesdash.com   (541) 323-0964

Bring the whole family out to compete or watch this multi-sport venue! Awards, medals, food, vendors and Deschutes Brewery beer are all part of the weekend fun!

Admission: Not Provided
Kid Friendly Event

Vendor Contact: Karin Roy karin@layitoutevents.com
# of Years Held: 12

7/18/2015 - 7/19/2015
Fire Festival & Concert
Ocean's Edge Wayside - Rockaway Beach, OR
www.rockawaybeach.net   (855) 233-6362

Admission: Not Provided

Vendor Contact: rbccsec@gmail.com

© *Festa Italiana Used With Permission*

7/18/2015 - 7/18/2015
Gresham Arts Festival
Historic Downtown Gresham
Gresham, OR

www.GreshamOregon.gov/ArtsFestival
503-618-2806

The Gresham Arts Festival is the community's biggest and best-loved event, consistently drawing thousands to Gresham's historic downtown every July to see and buy some of the best regional art around.

There's also live music, kids activities, and dining and shopping at over 150 stores, restaurants and cafes in the heart of Gresham.

This family-friendly event is free - including Gresham's new Children's Fountain, the only free splash pad for kids in East Multnomah County.

Free Admission
Kid Friendly Event
Hours: 9 a.m. to 5 p.m.

Vendor Contact: Kathy Kollenburn
kathy.kollenburn@greshamoregon.gov

Deadline: 6/30/15
# of Vendors: 150
Juried Event

Attendance: 12,000
# of Years Held: 14

7/18/2015 - 7/18/2015
Main Street Summerfest
Main Street - The Dalles, OR
www.thedallesmainstreet.org
(541) 296-1688

Main Street Summerfest takes place in Downtown The Dalles on July 18th, immediately following the Fort Dalles Days Pro Rodeo "50th Anniversary" Parade.

Federal St., from 1st to 4th will be closed, and the area filled with Live Music, a Food Court & Beer Garden, Street Vendors, Wild West Shoot Out, and more!

Totes with the Main Street Murder Mystery will be available. Explore our Downtown businesses to find the murderer, weapon, and location and be eligible for prizes!

The totes will also have discounts and other perks to thank the community for supporting our Downtown Businesses!

Free Admission
Kid Friendly Event
Hours: 10am - 5pm

Vendor Contact: tdmainstreet@gorge.net
7/18/2015 - 7/18/2015
Psychic Faire
Josephine County Fairgrounds - Grants Pass, OR
www.co.josephine.or.us   (541) 476-3215

It's a psychic faire, but you already knew that!

Admission: Not Provided

7/18/2015 - 7/19/2015
Southern Oregon Kite Festival
Kite Field at the Port of Brookings-Harbor
Brookings, OR
www.sokf.org   541-251-0498

The Southern Oregon Kite Festival is free and fun for ages! See nationally and internationally renowned kite flyers perform amazing routines choreographed to music on the kite field at the Port of Brookings-Harbor. Weekend activities include free children's kite building workshops and vendors selling eats, treats, and merchandise for the enjoyment of attendees. Free parking and free shuttles to the kite festival field are provided.

Free Admission
Kid Friendly Event
Hours: Sunday 10am-4pm

Vendor Contact: Mike Macdonald vendor@sokf.org
Deadline: 5/1/15   # of Vendors: 26
Not a Juried Event
Attendance: 10,000 +   # of Years Held: 23

7/18/2015 - 7/18/2015
Sunset Paddle
Tualatin Community Park - Tualatin, OR
www.eventbrite.com/o/tualatin-riverkeepers-
3912079195?s=24161027   (503) 218-2580

Join Tualatin Riverkeepers as we enjoy a summer evening paddle! The event launches from Tualatin Community Park, and requires a waiver form be completed. Limited space and reservations are required. The event is open to all members of the family.

Paid Admission
Kid Friendly Event

7/19/2015 - 7/19/2015
Forest Grove Concours d'Elegance
Pacific University Campus, 2043 College Way
Forest Grove, OR
www.forestgroveconcours.org   888-359-2530

Stroll around the beautiful campus of Pacific University
and enjoy 300 beautifully restored antique, classic,
sport, race and collector cars from several eras of
automotive history. Also enjoy a wine tasting booth, a
beer garden and music by the Tom Grant Band featuring
Shelly Rudolph. Save $3 on each on adult and senior
tickets by purchasing them in advance on line or by
calling 1.800.359.2510.

Paid Admission
Kid Friendly Event
Hours: Sunday 8:30 am - 4:30 pm

Vendor Contact: Jim Crisp
info@forestgroveconcours.org
Deadline: 6/30/15
# of Vendors: 300 Cars   Juried
EventAttendance: 6,000 to 10,000
# of Years Held: 43

7/19/2015 - 7/19/2015
The Blessing of the Animals
The Grotto - 8840 NE Skidmore St - Portland, OR
www.thegrotto.org   (503) 254-7371

Every year, this special event offers families and
individuals with pets, the opportunity to reflect upon the
positive impact animals have on our emotional and
physical well-being. Individuals of all faiths are invited
to bring their pet companion (properly restrained), to the
Grottom for a special blessing.

Kid Friendly Event
Hours: 2pm

7/21/2015 - 7/26/2015
Chief Joseph Days Ranch Rodeo
Joseph Rodeo Grounds - Joseph, OR
www.chiefjosephdays.org

Bucking horse stampeed, little buckaroo rodeo for kids with special needs, kiddie parade, live music & dancing, arts & crafts, food & refreshments and more!

Paid Admission

Vendor Contact: cjdays@eoni.com

7/21/2015 - 7/25/2015
Coos County Fair
900 4TH STREET - Myrtle Point, OR
www.co.coos.or.us   (541) 396-2200

Carnival, horse and livestock judging, Rodeo on July 24 and 25, 2015 with kids events beginning at 6:30 pm. Parade on the 25th beginning at 10am. Other misc entertainment with Friday and Saturday night dances beginning at 9:00 pm.

Paid Admission
Kid Friendly Event
Hours: T-Sat 8am - 10pm
          Exhibit buildings are open from 10 - 10

Vendor Contact: Debbie James djames@co.coos.or.us
Deadline: 7/20/15   # of Vendors: 65
Not a Juried Event   Attendance: 28771
# of Years Held: 103

I am summer, come to lure you away from your computer...Come dance on my fresh grass, dig your toes into my beaches.
~~Oriana Green, @NatureSpirits

7/22/2015 - 7/25/2015
Hood River County Fair
Hood River Fairgrounds - Hood River, OR
www.hoodriverfair.org   (541) 354-2865

Paid Admission
Kid Friendly Event

Vendor Contact: hrfair@hrecn.net
# of Vendors: 80
Attendance: 25000   # of Years Held: 88

7/22/2015 - 7/26/2015
Jackson County Fair
Jackson County Expo & Fairgrounds - Central Point, OR
www.attheexpo.com   (541) 774-8270

Paid Admission
Kid Friendly Event

Vendor Contact: Dave Koellermeier
# of Vendors: 102
Attendance: 150000

7/22/2015 - 7/25/2015
Jefferson County Fair
Jefferson County Fairgrounds - Madras, OR
www.jcfairgrounds.org   (541) 325-5050

Paid Admission
Kid Friendly Event

Vendor Contact: Sandy Forman
sandy.forman@co.jefferson.or.us
# of Vendors: 50
Attendance: 20000
# of Years Held: 82

7/22/2015 - 7/26/2015
Lane County Fair
Fairgrounds - Eugene, OR
www.atthefair.com   (541) 682-4282

Rides!   Food!   Animals!   Vendors!   Exhibits!   Rockin'
Concerts! Great Entertainment! The annual Lane County
Fair has something for the whole family.   2015 Concert
Series: Wed: Joan Jett and the Blackhearts, Thurs: Brett
Eldgredge. Fri: Under the Sun Tour (featuring Uncle
Kracker, Mark McGrath with Sugar Ray, Kevin Griffin Of
Better Than Ezra And Eve 6), Sat: Theory of a Deadman,
Sun: Easton Corbin. Check the website for tickets, tons
more information and daily specials.

Free Admission
Kid Friendly Event
Hours: Wed-Sat 11am-11pm
          Sun 11am-8pm

Vendor Contact: Ron Eggleston
vendors@atthefair.com
Deadline: 7/15/15
# of Vendors: 200   Juried Event
Attendance: 100000
# of Years Held: 96

O beautiful for spacious skies,
For amber waves of grain.
For purple mountains majesties,
Above the fruited plain!
America! America! God shed his grace on thee,
And crown thy good with brother hood,
From sea to shining sea!
~~ Lyrics – America the Beautiful
Words by katharine Lee Bates; Melody by Samuel Ward

7/22/2015 - 7/26/2015
Oregon Brewers Festival
Waterfront Park - Portland, OR
www.oregonbrewfest.com

This festival is the quintessential celebration of craft beers! Come spend a sunny July afternoon, sipping suds with friends along the banks of the Willamette River, with Mt Hood and the Portland skyline as your backdrop. From Belgians to Blondes, Pales, Pilsners, Saisons and Wits, you'll see why this is one of the world's best loved craft beer festivals!

Admission: Not Provided

Vendor Contact: Chris Crabb
chris@oregonbrewfest.com

# of Vendors: 15   Attendance: 80000
# of Years Held: 28

7/22/2015 - 7/26/2015
Oregon High Desert Classic II
62895 Hamby Rd - Bend, OR
www.oregonhighdesertclassics.org (541) 389-1409

Admission: Not Provided

Vendor Contact: Zoe Gilbert zgilbert@jbarj.org

7/23/2015 - 7/26/2015
Newberg Old Fashioned Festival
Memorial Park - Newberg, OR
www.newbergoldfashionedvestival.com

Carnival, car show, brews & BBQ, parades, stage entertainment, arts & crafts, food vendors and more!

Admission: Not Provided
Kid Friendly Event
Vendor Contact: Jessica Fettig (503) 537-1230, ext. 2

7/24/2015 - 7/26/2015
ArtSplash Art Show and Sale
Lake Commons, 8325 SW Nyberg
Street - Tualatin, OR

www.tualatinoregon.gov/recreation/artsplash-art-show-and-sale   503-691-3076

Are you looking for some great art, jewelry, ceramics, music and fun? Come out to the City of Tualatin's ArtSplash Art Show and Sale July 24-26, 2015. Northwest artists will be showcasing their talents in watercolor, acrylic, oil, jewelry, glass, and more.

There will be activities throughout the weekend including a concert Friday night featuring R&B great Curtis Salgado and New Horizon Big Band of Tualatin on Saturday night.

Free Admission
Kid Friendly Event
Hours: Friday Noon-9:00pm Saturday 11:00am-9:00pm
          Sunday 10:00am-4:00pm

# of Years Held: 20

© *Stux* *All Free Download*

7/24/2015 - 7/25/2015
Balloons Over Bend Children's Festival
Summitt High - Bend, OR
www.balloonsoverbend.com   (541) 323-0964

Bringing families, visitors and businesses together in a community celebration that has something for every generation to enjoy!   Live music, food, 15 hot air balloons are launched, handcrafted arts, kids activities, kite flying, chalk art, hot air baloons night glow, beer garden for the older generation and more!

Admission: Not Provided
Kid Friendly Event

Vendor Contact: Emily Arredondo
info@layitoutevents.com   # of Years Held: 12

7/24/2015 - 7/25/2015
Blackberry Jam Festival
Rolling Rock Park - Lowell, OR
www.blackberryjamfestival.com   (866) 516-5534

This wholesome community event features everything berry! Plenty of great music, unique handcrafted arts of work and delicious food!   Other features include a car show, fishing derby, quilt show, parade and plenty of fun for the young and young at heart! Bring your appetite--- - there's even a pie eating contest!

Free Admission
Kid Friendly Event
Hours: Fri: 5-11pm; Sat:10am-11pm; Sun: 11am-5pm

Vendor Contact: Maureen Weathers
info@blackberryjamfestival.com
Deadline: 7/1/15   # of Vendors: 45
Attendance: 4500   # of Years Held: 21

7/24/2015 - 7/25/2015
Estacada Summer Celebration
Broadway and 4th St. Estacada Oregon - Estacada, OR
www.estacadasc.org   (503) 939-5101

This annual, free, music and arts festival celebrates 15 years. Friday night´s kick-off Music Crawl showcases local musicians performing in downtown businesses and JC & The Water Walkers on the main stage.

Performances take place all day Saturday, featuring a variety of well-known regional musicians: NW Women in Blues, Hurqalya, Melanie Roy Band, Unit Souzou Taiko Drumming.

A juried street art fair, hands-on art activities for children, food vendors, a growing family of giant puppets, circus skills workshops, street labyrinth painting, and totem-pole carving demonstrations.

Celebrate the annual painting of a large outdoor mural by the Artback Artists, who will repaint Early Trains of Estacada .

Free Admission
Kid Friendly Event
Hours: Friday 6pm -10pm Saturday 10am-10:30pm

Vendor Contact: Cherie Lingle cheriegl@aol.com
Deadline: 6/15/15
# of Vendors: 30   Juried Event

7/24/2015 - 8/21/2015
Flicks on the Bricks
Pioneer Courthouse Square - Downtown - Portland, OR

Movies show at dusks on 7/24, 31, 8/7, 14, and 21 only

Admission: Not Provided
Kid Friendly Event

7/24/2015 - 7/26/2015
Garibaldi Days
Memorial Lumberman's Park - Garibaldi, OR
www.visitgaribaldi.com

Admission: Not Provided

Vendor Contact: Lori Wilcox (503) 322-0206
loriwilcox2285@centurylink.net

7/24/2015 - 7/26/2015
Garibaldi Days 2015
Hwy 101 thru Garibaldi - Garibaldi, OR
www.visitgaribaldi.com/garibaldi-days-0
(503) 322-3327

This festival kicks off on Friday with scheduled trips by the Oregon Coast Scenic Railway from Garibaldi to Rockaway Beach.

The annual parade begins at 11am on Saturday. Following the parade... live entertainment, dozens of vendors offering a variety of food and refreshments, and artisans selling their handcrafted wares.

Fireworks caps the day's activities on Saturday evening.

Admission: Not Provided
Kid Friendly Event
Hours: Fri & Sat: 10am-6pm;
        Sun: 10am-3pm

Vendor Contact: Mary DeLoria mary@ci.garibaldi.or.us
Deadline: 6/15/15
# of Vendors: 60
Attendance: 10000   # of Years Held: 55

7/24/2015 - 7/25/2015
Sandy Shores Gift Expo
Seaside Convention Center - Seaside, OR
www.gpsfundraisersandevents.com (425) 343-3233

Admission: Not Provided

Vendor Contact:
gpsfundraisersandevents@gmail.com
# of Years Held: 1

7/25/2015 - 7/25/2015
7th NW Annual Book Festival
Pioneer Courthouse Square - Portland, OR
www.nwbookfestival.com   503-913-6006

Meet over 100 critically acclaimed, well-known authors in person, get an autograph, ask questions, and get inspired!

Let's keep books alive! A fun-filled family day, and it's free!   Event will be held once again at the historical Pioneer Courthouse Square in downtown Portland, considered to be one of the busiest most visited sites by city dwellers and tourists from all over the country.

There will be books on, Poetry, Romance, Spiritual/ Self-Help, Children's books, History, Memoirs, Horror/Thriller, Humor/Satire, Travel, Young Adult, Fantasy, Art, and so much more. Visit us online for list of authors, publishers and bookstores.

Free Admission
Kid Friendly Event
Hours: Saturday from 11 to 5pm. One day only.

Vendor Contact: Veronica Esagui
Handson13@hotmail.com
Deadline: 6/27/15
# of Vendors: 65   Not a Juried Event
Attendance: 3200   # of Years Held: 7

7/25/2015 - 7/25/2015
Beaverton International Celebration
THPRD Howard M Terpenning Complex - Beaverton, OR
www.beavertonoregon.gov   (503) 526-2559

Fun, family-friendly event showcasing the many cultures through the arts!   Music, dance, interactive activities, food, art and more!

Free Admission
Kid Friendly Event

Vendor Contact: events@beavertonoregon.gov

7/25/2015 - 7/25/2015
Division/Clinton Street Fair & Parade
Division/Clinton Streets - Portland, OR
www.divisionclinton.com   (503) 771-3428

Free Admission
Kid Friendly Event

Vendor Contact: Nancy Chapin nchapin@tsgpdx.com
# of Vendors: 125

Sun in the Sand © Petr Kratochvil
All Free Downloads

7/25/2015 - 7/26/2015
Great Oregon Summer Steam Up
3995 Brooklake Rd NE - Brooks, OR
www.antiquepowerland.com   (503) 393-2424

Includes a parade with vintage tractors, trucks and automobiles. The steam powered sawmill operates four times a day, and the trolley tours the site perimeter all four days. Come learn about the past at the Great Oregon Steam-Up!

Admission: Not Provided
Kid Friendly Event

# of Vendors: 200   Attendance: 22000   # of Years Held: 45

7/25/2015 - 7/26/2015
Hoops at the Beach
Lincoln City Outlets - Lincoln City, OR
www.oregoncoast.org

Admission: Not Provided
Kid Friendly Event

Vendor Contact:
info@allwaystravelingandpromotions.com

I drifted into a soft summertime nap under the shade of a tree one hot July day… serenaded by the strings of a cricket's song, with the slow gurgle of the brook accompanying with its steady, sweet beat. I hear a little frog join in the melody of summer and I grow drowsy with warm dreams of summertimes past.
~~Catherine Pittman © 2015

What is a perfect summer day?
It is seeing the bright blue summer sky,
Hearing the melodies of nature all sing in harmony,
And feeling the sweet summer sun kiss my face.
These are the joys of the perfect summer day!
~~Catherine Pittman © 2015

7/25/2015 - 7/25/2015
Oregon's First City Celebration
Downtown - Oregon City, OR
www.downtownoregoncity.org/firstcity/
(971) 202-1606

This signature event is the largest citywide celebration of Oregon City's legacy as the first city of the Oregon Territory. Includes kids activity zone, heritage village, craft beer and wine garden, and downtown's weekly Saturday artisan market.

Free Admission
Kid Friendly Event

Vendor Contact: Jessica Gago
jessica@downtownoregoncity.org
Deadline: 7/1/15   # of Vendors: 100
Attendance: 5000   # of Years Held: 6

7/25/2015 - 7/26/2015
Portland Craft Fair
Rejuvenation 1100 SE Grand Ave - Portland, OR
www.renegadecraft.com   (773) 227-2707

Admission: Not Provided
Hours: 11am - 6pm

Vendor Contact: duggan@renegadecraft.com
Deadline: 6/27/15   Juried Event

Child in the Meadow
© *George Hodan*
All Free Downloads

7/25/2015 - 7/25/2015
Santiam SummerFest 2015
Pioneer Park - Stayton, OR
www.staytonsublimitychamber.org/events/santia
m-summerfest/

Admission: Not Provided
Kid Friendly Event
Hours: 9am - 3pm

Vendor Contact: ssoc@wvi.com
Attendance: 10000   # of Years Held: 20

7/25/2015 - 7/26/2015
Sisters Arts & Crafts Festival
Sisters City Creekside Park - Sisters, OR
www.centraloregonshows.com   (541) 420-0279

This special event fundraiser benefits The Make-A-Wish
Foundation of Oregon.

Paid Admission
Kid Friendly Event

Vendor Contact: centraloregonshows@gmail.com
# of Vendors: 85   Juried Event
Attendance: 10000   # of Years Held: 15

7/25/2015 - 7/25/2015
Stayton SummerFest Car Show
Pioneer Park - Stayton, OR
www.staytonsublimitychamber.org/events/santia
m-summerfest/

Paid Car Registration
Kid Friendly Event
Hours: 9am - 3pm

Vendor Contact: Ron Sowerby (503) 881-8318
stroscars@wvi.com

7/26/2015 - 7/26/2015
Lents Street Fair
SE 91st from Foster to Reedway - Portland, OR
www.lentsstreetfair.com

Free basic bike repair, carnival games, bouncy house, arts and crafts exhibits, live music, greet food and beer, classic cars, a parade to honor our history and more!

Free Admission
Kid Friendly Event
Hours: Noon - 5pm

Vendor Contact: amanda@ilovelents.com

7/26/2015 - 7/26/2015
North Powder Huckleberry Festival
"Huckleberry Fun!"
Heart of North Powder - North Powder, OR

Huckleberry sundaes, huckleberry dessert competition, activities for kids, mud volleyball tournament, street dance, parade, art & craft vendors, food vendors and more!

Admission: Not Provided
Kid Friendly Event

Vendor Contact: Bev Bigler bibig@eoni.com

Water Color Lake Swan
© Leslie Pittman

7/26/2015 - 7/26/2015
Old Car Sunday & BBQ
726 W. Oak Street - Lebanon, OR
www.firstassemblylebanonoregon.com
(541) 259-1265

Old Car Show Sunday July 26th, 2015, Come enjoy the day! BBQ lunch $6 per. Includes: BBQ Hamburg (all the fixins), Potato Salad, Beans & Drink. Pop & or Water $1.00 ea.

Cars, Motorcycles and Trucks are Welcome ! Best of All Free Registration for All Vehicles.

Free Admission
Kid Friendly Event
Hours: Sunday July 26th, 2015 8am-3pm

# of Years Held: 4th year

7/26/2015 - 7/26/2015
Parents' Day Celebration
McEwen Depot - Baker City, OR
www.sumptervalleyrailroad.org

We celebrate parents' day by providing a round trip Family Pass for the price of a one-way fare. Or a round trip adult ticket for the price of a one-way fare with accompanying child from infant to 16.

Paid Admission
Kid Friendly Event

Vendor Contact: info@sumptervalleyrailroad.org

7/27/2015 - 7/31/2015
Critter Camp for Ages 5 1/2 - 10
Spark Arts Center, 1805 NE Cesar Chavez Blvd, Portland,
OR 97212 - Portland, OR
www.sparkartscenter.com   (503) 281-6757

Who can resist a fuzzy little critter and who says they
have to be realistic? Create critters both real and
imaginary as we work with clay, paper mache and hand
sewing.

Paid Admission
Kid Friendly Event
Hours: M-F, 12:30-4:30

7/27/2015 - 7/31/2015
Critter Camp for Ages 5 1/2 - 10
Spark Arts Center, 1805 NE Cesar Chavez Blvd, Portland,
OR 97212 - Portland, OR
www.sparkartscenter.com   (503) 281-6757

Who can resist a fuzzy little critter and who says they
have to be realistic? Create critters both real and
imaginary as we work with clay, paper mache and hand
sewing.

Paid Admission
Kid Friendly Event
Hours: M-F, 12:30-4:30

7/28/2015 - 8/1/2015
Clatsop County Fair
Clatsop County Fairgrounds - Astoria, OR
www.clatsopfairgrounds.com   (503) 325-4600

Paid Admission
Kid Friendly Event

Vendor Contact: Gary gfriedman@co.clatsop.or.us
# of Vendors: 45   Attendance: 18,000

7/28/2015 - 8/11/2015
Concerts in the Park - Kenton
Kenton Park - N Kilpatrick & Delaware - Portland, OR

Free Admission
Hours: Tuesdays - 6:30 pm

7/28/2015 - 8/1/2015
Malheur County Fair
Malheur County Fairgrounds - Ontario, OR
www.malheurcountyfair.com   (541) 889-3431

Paid Admission
Kid Friendly Event

Vendor Contact: Janeen Kressly mcfair@fmtc.com
# of Vendors: 57   Attendance: 25000

7/29/2015 - 8/1/2015
Benton County Fair & Rodeo
Benton County Fairgrounds - Corvallis, OR
www.bentoncountyfair.net   (541) 766-6521

Paid Admission
Kid Friendly Event

Vendor Contact: Lonny Wunder info@co.benton.or.us
# of Vendors: 100   Attendance: 55000

7/29/2015 - 8/2/2015
Deschutes County Fair & Rodeo
Deschutes County Fairgrounds - Redmond, OR
www.expo.deschutes.org   (541) 548-2711

Paid Admission
Kid Friendly Event

Vendor Contact: Dan Despotopulos
dand@deschutes.org   Deadline: 7/15/15
Attendance: 250,000

7/29/2015 - 8/2/2015
DuneFest 2015
Salmon Harbor Dr - Winchester Bay, OR
www.dunefest.com   (541) 914-8402

Admission: Not Provided
Kid Friendly Event

Vendor Contact: Michael Allen
dunefestpromoter@gmail.com
Attendance: 1,500

7/29/2015 - 8/1/2015
Union County Fair
Union County Fairgrounds - La Grande, OR
www.union-county.org/fair/   (541) 963-1011

~ Talent Show
~ Parade
~ Live Entertainment
~ Kids Activities
~ Carnival & more!

Paid Admission
Kid Friendly Event

Vendor Contact: Nan Bigej nbigej@gmail.com
# of Vendors: 30   Attendance: 30,000

Indian Summer
© *Larisa Koshkina*
All Free Downloads

7/29/2015 - 8/1/2015
Yamhill County Fair
Yamhill County Fairgrounds - McMinnville, OR
www.co.yamhill.or.us/fair   (503) 434-7524

Paid Admission
Kid Friendly Event
Hours: 10am-11pm

Vendor Contact: fair@co.yamhill.or.us
# of Vendors: 50   Attendance: 30000
# of Years Held: 161

7/29/2015 - 8/1/2015
Yamhill County Fair
2070 NE Lafayette Ave. - McMinnville, OR
www.co.yamhill.or.us/fair   (503) 434-7524

Oregon's Oldest County Fair featuring concerts by Lonestar, Joe Nichols, Aaron Tippin and Warrant. All entertainment included with admission - concerts, rodeo, demo derby and more! Preferred concert seating for only $7 in addition to admission.

Great food, carnival and vendors. 4-H and FFA exhibits including youth livestock auction. Don't miss 'Summer's Biggest Party' July 29-August 1 in McMinnville!

Paid Admission
Kid Friendly Event
Hours: Wednesday-Thursday 10 am - 11 pm Friday-Saturday 10 am - 12 midnight

Vendor Contact: Al Westhoff fair@co.yamhill.or.us
Deadline: 6/15/15   # of Vendors: 35
Juried Event   Attendance: 38,000
# of Years Held: 100+

7/30/2015 - 8/2/2015
Funky Junk Sisters Rebel Junk
Washington County Fairgrounds - Hillsboro, OR
www.funkyjunksisters.com

Two Weekends: 7/30 & 31 and 8/1 & 2
Vendor Contact: funkyjunksisters@live.com

7/30/2015 - 8/1/2015
Sweet Home Arts & Crafts Festival
Sweet Home High School - Sweet Home, OR
www.oregonjamboree.com/arts-crafts/
(541) 367-8800

Featuring juried artisans presending handmade arts and crafts from local and regional artisans.

Free Admission
Hours: Fri & Sat: 9am-8pm; Sun: 9am-5pm

Vendor Contact: vendors@oregonjamboree.com
Deadline: 3/31/15   # of Vendors: 65
Juried Event
Attendance: 8000   # of Years Held: 14

7/30/2015 - 8/2/2015
Washington County Fair
Washington Co. Fairgrounds - Hillsboro, OR
www.bigfairfun.com   (503) 648-1416

The best carnival rides around, farm animals, amazing food booths, great live stage entertainment... You'll find something for everyone in your family!

Paid Admission
Kid Friendly Event
Hours: 10am-11pm daily

Vendor Contact: Leah Perkins-Hagele
generaloffices@faircomplex.com
# of Vendors: 315   Attendance: 100,000

7/31/2015 - 8/2/2015
Cape Blanco Country Music Festival
Cape Blanco State Park - Sixes, OR
www.capeblancofestival.com   (541) 345-9263

Country music fans will find an inviting home at Cape Blanco Country Music Festival!

Paid Admission

Vendor Contact: info@capeblancofestival.com
Attendance: 15,000

7/31/2015 - 8/2/2015
Tualatin Crawfish Festival
Tualatin Commons - Tualatin, OR
www.tualatincrawfishfestival.com (503) 730-0256

Paid Admission
Kid Friendly Event

Vendor Contact: haskin.bryce.l@gmail.com

I love summertime more than anything else in the world. That is the only thing that gets me through the winter... knowing that summer is going to be there.
~~Jack McBrayer, American Actor

Summer afternoon—summer afternoon; to me those have always been the two most beautiful words in the English language.
~~Henry James 1843 - 1916

Let us dance in the sun, wearing wild flowers in our hair.
~~Susan Polis Schutz, American Author

August 2015

8/1/2015 - 8/2/2015
ArtBurst NorthWest
ArtBurst NorthWest-Marylhurst, OR
www.artburstnw.org

ArtBurst NorthWest is a fine arts and crafts festival located on the grounds of beautiful Marylhurst University. August 1 - 2, 2015. ArtBurst NW showcases the work of more than 100 Pacific Northwest artists in all media.

ArtBurst NorthWest is produced by artists for artists, open for all to attend, and celebrating the arts and creativity of the region with the accompaniment of great food, music, shaded dining and lounging in a relaxed outdoor atmosphere.

Free Admission
No Kid's Activities
Hours: Saturday, August 1, 10 am-6 pm
            Sunday, August 2, 10 am-5 pm

Vendor Contact: info@artburstnw.org
Deadline: 6/15/15   # of Vendors: 100   Juried Event
Attendance: 9000   # of Years Held: 16

Oh, the summer night,
Has a smile of light,
And she sits on a sapphire throne.
~~ Barry Cornwall, English Poet 1787-1874

8/1/2015 – 8/2/2015
Festival of Art in Stout Park
433 Oak Street in Stout Park surrounding Manley Art
Cntr - Brookings, OR
www.wildriverscoastart.com   (541) 469-9522

Festival of Art in Stout Park includes 70 juried artisans in lovely park setting, plein air painting, food court, wine and micro-brew. Local musicians provide entertainment. Stout Mountain Railroad has trains running throughout the weekend. August 1, 10:00 - 5:00 and August 2, 10:00 - 4:00. Located one block off of Highway 101.

Free Admission
Kid Friendly Event
Hours: Saturday 10am - 5 pm; Sunday 10 am - 4pm

Vendor Contact: Violet Burton burtonique@gmail.com
Deadline: 3/31/15   # of Vendors: 70   Juried Event
Attendance: 2,000   # of Years Held: 3

8/1/2015 - 8/2/2015
Pathways to Transformation
Yachats Commons Bldg - Yachats, OR
www.chucklingcherubs.com   (541) 547-4664

Featuring the largest array of holistic health practitioners, psychic readers, health & wellness products and visionary arts and crafts under one roof!

Admission: Donations Welcome
No Kid's Activities
Hours: Sat: 10am-7pm; Sun: 9am-5pm

Vendor Contact: cherubs@peak.org
# of Vendors: 60   Attendance: 2000
# of Years Held: 20

8/1/2015 - 8/1/2015
Soulful Giving Blanket Concert
Yoshida's Gardenview Estate, 29330 SE Stark St
Troutdale, OR
www.soulfulgiving.org   503-731-3729

Prepare to spread your blankets and sand chairs under shady fir trees and enjoy a fun-filled day along the scenic Sandy River in Troutdale, Oregon. This is the Soulful Giving Foundation's 5th annual "21 and over" music, wine, beer, food and art event - in other words...the Soulful Giving Blanket Concert benefiting Providence Cancer Center and Randall Children's Hospital. Free parking and shuttle service at Mt. Hood Community College and downtown near the Crowne Plaza Hotel. For more information and ticket sales, visit www.soulfulgiving.org.

Admission - $25, Premier Admission (food & beverage tokens included) - $50, and VIP Admission (limo, expedited entry, food & beverage tokens & commemorative gift) - $100.

No Kid's Activities
Hours: Saturday 11:30am - 8:30pm

Vendor Contact: Diane VanLaningham
Dianem.Van@gmail.com
Deadline: 5/5/2015   # of Vendors: 32
Not a Juried Event   Attendance: 3,000+
# of Years Held: 5

8/1/2015 - 8/1/2015
Sublimity Car Show
Sublimity Harvest Festival Grounds - Sublimity, OR
www.staytonsublimitychamber.org/events/santia
m-summerfest/

Paid Car Registration
Kid Friendly Event
Hours: 9am - 3pm

Vendor Contact: Russ Strohmeyerat (503) 930-0976
stroscars@wvi.com

8/1/2015 - 8/2/2015
Summer Festival
Rice Northwest Museum of Rocks & Minerals
Hillsboro, OR
www.ricenorthwestmuseum.org/2015/05/30/201
5-summer-festival-august-1-2/   503-647-2418

Summer Festival at the Rice NW Museum of Rocks and
Minerals is an outdoor event including vendors with
minerals, gems, fossils, jewelry, gold panning, geode
cutting, and kids activities. There will be local food
available for purchase, live music, and an appearance by
Fred and Wilma Flintstone both days. A silent auction,
raffles, and door prizes will be held throughout the day.
Admission is $5 for adults, free for 17 years old and
under.

Paid Admission
Kid Friendly Event
Hours: Sat-Sun 10am-5pm

Vendor Contact: Julian Gray
info@ricenorthwestmuseum.org
Deadline: 6/30/15
# of Vendors: 30   Not a Juried Event
Attendance: 1200   # of Years Held: 11

8/1/2015 - 8/8/2015
Wallowa County Fair
668 NW First, Enterprise, OR -
Enterprise, OR
www.facebook.com/WallowaCou
ntyFair?ref=hl 541-426-4097

Located in beautiful Wallowa Valley, the Wallowa County Fair has been operating since 1907, showcasing youth projects and community member's skills. 4H Dog and Horse Shows start the week, with Open Class exhibits and vendors opening on Wednesday. The week finishes with a 4H/FFA Stock Sale the final Saturday evening. Enjoy the rural setting, animals, and events at the 2015 Wallowa County Fair, featuring "Rabbits, Ribbons, and Roses."

Free Admission
Kid Friendly Event
Hours: Sat., Aug 1, 8 am - 2 pm W-F 10 am - 7 pm
         Sat., Aug. 8,10 am - 7 pm

Vendor Contact: Gretchen Piper
wallowacountyfair@gmail.com
Deadline: 7/7/15   # of Vendors: 8
Not a Juried Event
Attendance: 3000   # of Years Held: 108

8/2/2015 - 8/2/2015
Fashion Expo
Pioneer Courthouse Square - Downtown - Portland, OR

This annual fashion show features more than just a fashion show!

Free Admission
Hours: 11am - 7pm

8/4/2015 - 8/9/2015
Wheeler County Fair
Wheeler County Fairgrounds - Fossil, OR (541) 763-4560

Paid Admission
Kid Friendly Event

Vendor Contact: wheeler002@centurytel.net
# of Vendors: 50   Attendance: 2500
# of Years Held: 103

8/5/2015 - 8/8/2015
Baker County Fair
Baker County Fairgrounds - Baker City, OR
www.bakercounty.org/fair   (541) 523-7881

Paid Admission
Kid Friendly Event
Hours: 9am - 9pm

Vendor Contact: Angie Turner
bakerfair@bakercounty.org # of Vendors: 31
Attendance: 8000   # of Years Held: 87

8/5/2015 - 8/26/2015
Concerts in the Park - Ventura
Ventura Park - Portland, OR

Free Admission
Hours: Thursdays - 6:30 pm

Shell in the Sand © Tom Genovese

8/5/2015 - 8/8/2015
Crook County Fair
Crook County Fairgrounds - Prineville, OR
www.crookcountyfairgrounds.com (541) 447-6575

This year marks the 112th Crook County Fair. The fair is Free Admission/Free Parking. Entertainment this year will include Brady Goss band on Wednesday night, 2nd Annual Battle of the Bands Thursday, Parmalee (paid admission) Friday, and Countryfied Friday and Saturday! Daily we will have Butler Amusements Midway, Something Ridiculous, JJ Entertainers, Western Express Railroad, Puzzlemania, Mechanical Bull, Euro Bungee, Archery Tag, Corn is Everywhere plus tons more fun things.

Free Admission
Kid Friendly Event
Hours: Wednesday 5pm-10pm Thursday 10am-10pm
Friday 10am-10pm Saturday 10am-10pm

Vendor Contact: Micaela Halvorson
ccfgstaff@co.crook.or.us
Deadline: 7/24/15
# of Vendors: 12 Food, 40 Craft/Commercial
Juried Event
Attendance: 25000   # of Years Held: 112

8/5/2015 - 8/8/2015
Douglas County Fair
Douglas County Fairgrounds - Roseburg, OR
www.co.douglas.or.us   (541) 440-4396

Admission: Not Provided
Kid Friendly Event

Vendor Contact: bsmayber@co.douglas.or.us
# of Vendors: 200   Attendance: 60000

8/5/2015 - 9/9/2015
Sunsets in the Garden
The Oregon Garden - Silverton, OR
www.oregongarden.org/events/sunsets-in-the-garden/   503-874-8100

Sunsets in the Garden, presented by Columbia Bank, is a great way to enjoy a summer evening after-hours in the Garden with live music, beer and wine tasting, tram tours and sunset viewing. The event is an extension of Garden hours on Wednesday evenings, August 5 - September 9. Regular Garden admission applies: Adults $11, Seniors (60+) $9, Students (12-17) $8, Children 5-11 $5, Children 4 & Under Free, Garden Members Free

Paid Admission
Kid Friendly Event
Hours: 6:30 - 9pm

Vendor Contact: Mary Ridderbusch-Shearer
info@oregongarden.org
Deadline: April   # of Vendors: varies
Not a Juried Event
Attendance: 50-100/event   # of Years Held: 4

8/5/2015 - 8/8/2015
Tillamook County Fair
Tillaook County Fairgrounds - Tillamook, OR
www.tillamookfair.com   (503) 842-2272

4-H/FFA Exhibits, animal displays, demolition derby, talent shows, pig-n-ford races, horse racing, courtyard entertainment, kids activities, food and artisan vendors and much more!

Paid Admission
Kid Friendly Event

Vendor Contact: tillamookfair@tillamookfair.com

8/6/2015 - 8/20/2015
Concerts in the Park - Berrydale
Berrydale Park - Se 92nd & Taylor - Portland, OR

Free Admission
Hours: Thursdays - 6:30 pm

8/6/2015 - 8/13/2015
Concerts in the Park - Couch
Couch Park - NW 20th & Glisan - Portland, OR

Free Admission
Hours: Thursdays - 6:30 pm

8/6/2015 - 8/8/2015
Polk County Fair
520 S. Pacific Hwy W - Rickreall, OR
www.co.polk.or.us/fair   503-623-3048

Good old Fashion County Fair - Rough Stock Rodeo, Truck & Tractor Pulls, ATV Rodeo, Free Monster Truck rides on Sat. plus lots of animal and static exhibits by 4H/FFA and open class. Free kids area. Good food & Family Fun!!

Parking is free

Paid Admission Adults $8.00 Youth 11 - 15 yrs. $5.00
                kids 10 & under free.
Kid Friendly Event
Hours: Thurs. & Fri. - 10am - 10pm Sat. 10am - 11pm

Vendor Contact: Linda Friedow
friedow.linda@co.polk.or.us
Deadline: 8/1/15
# of Vendors: 102   Juried Event
Attendance: 22000   # of Years Held: 89

8/7/2015 - 8/9/2015
Bite of Oregon
Portland Waterfront Park - Portland, OR
www.biteoforegon.com   (503) 248-0600

Paid Admission
Kid Friendly Event

# of Years Held: 32

8/7/2015 - 8/21/2015
Concerts in the Park - Lovejoy
Lovejoy Fountain Park - SW 3rd & Harrison, Downtown -
Portland, OR

Free Admission
Hours: Fridays - 6:30 pm

8/7/2015 - 8/9/2015
Homer Davenport Community Festival
Coolidge-McClaine City Park - Silverton, OR
www.homerdavenport.com   (503) 873-5615

This great community event features a classic fun-run,
live music, arts and crafts, food, fun in the park, a
parade and the world-famous Davenport Races down
Main St.

Free Admission
Kid Friendly Event
Hours: Fri & Sat: 10am-8pm; Sun: 10am-6pm

Vendor Contact: homer@homerdavenport.com
# of Vendors: 75   Juried Event
Attendance: 9000   # of Years Held: 35

8/7/2015 - 8/9/2015
North Plains Elephant Garlic festival
Jessie Mays Community Center & Park - 30975 NW
Hillcrest Avenue - North Plains, OR
www.funstinks.com   503-449-5447

North Plains Elephant Garlic Festival was rated 10th best
Garlic Festival in the World by Travel Magazine a few
years ago. This is a FREE event to the public. Featuring
a Beer and Wine Garden, Live Music, 65 hand made Art
Vendors, 20 Food Vendors with lots of garlicky goodness,
Raw garlic for sale. Parade, Kids play area, North Plains
Library Book Sale, car show. Come join us for the 18th
Annual Elephant Garlic Festival!

Free Admission
Kid Friendly Event
Hours: Fri noon - 11 pm art vendors to 8 pm
            Sat 10 am - 11 pm art vendors to 8pm
            Sun August 9th 10 am - 6 pm

Vendor Contact: sherrie simmons
sherrie.funstinks@gmail.com
Deadline: 6/1/15   Juried Event
Attendance: 15,000 - 20,000   # of Years Held: 18

8/7/2015 - 8/9/2015
Oregon Garlic Festival
Sunset Park - Banks, OR
www.funstinks.com   (503) 449-5447

Free Admission
Kid Friendly Event

Vendor Contact: Sherrie sherrie.funstinks@gmail.com
Deadline: 3/16/15   # of Vendors: 60   Juried Event
Attendance: 30,000   # of Years Held: 18

8/7/2015 - 8/8/2015
Quilts by the Sea
Newport Recreation Center, 225 SE Avery St.
Newport, OR
www.OregonCoastalQuilters.org   541-563-5540

2015 QUILT SHOW: Quilts by the Sea Presented by the Oregon Coastal Quilters Guild, Celebrating 25 years at the coast with over 300 quilts made by Coastal Quilters from traditional bed quilts to fabulous art quilts.

There is something for everyone! Plus small quilt auction for charity, variety of vendors, demonstrations, antique quilts, boutique with many hand-made items and fabric, children's activity corner, raffle quilt and more!

Paid Admission
Kid Friendly Event
Hours: Friday, Aug 7th, 10-6 Saturday, Aug 8th 9-4

Vendor Contact: Janet Baldwin
janetbaldwin45@gmail.com
Deadline: Until Filled   # of Vendors: 26
Not a Juried Event   # of Years Held: 25

8/7/2015 - 8/7/2015
Sandy Summer First Friday
Downtown Main Street - Sandy, OR
www.sandymainstreet.org   (503) 489-2173

Admission: Not Provided
Hours: 5-8pm

Vendor Contact: Jennifer Marks jmarks@ci.sandy.or.us

8/7/2015 - 8/9/2015
Sunriver Art Faire

The Village at Sunriver - Sunriver, OR
www.sunriverartfaire.com   877-269-2580

The Sixth Annual Sunriver Art Faire is one of the premier summer art events in Central Oregon. The juried Faire showcases 60+ artists including works in ceramics, glass, jewelry, painting, photography, sculpture, textiles, woodworking and mixed media.

Professional entertainment plays all three days, a center for young artists is available, and food can be purchased in the Village.

Net proceeds from the Faire are distributed to nonprofit community agencies serving basic needs of Deschutes County children and families.

Free Admission
Kid Friendly Event
Hours: Friday & Saturday 10am-6pm
         Sunday 10am-4pm

Vendor Contact: sunriverartfaire@gmail.com
Deadline: 3/1/15
# of Vendors: 73   Juried Event
Attendance: 10,000+   # of Years Held: Six

Beautiful and graceful, varied and enchanting, small but approchable, butterfliest lead you to the sunny side of life. And everyone deserves a little sunshine!
~~Jeffrey Glassberg

Buttercups in the August sunshine are like little cups of gold,
Dasies and sunflowers rise with bowing head towards the sun,
Violets of majestic blue creep within the shadow of the tree,
Butterflies dance from flower-to-flower,
Fluttering on the summer breeze and never a care in the world.
~~ Catherine Pittman © 2015

8/8/2015 - 8/8/2015
Alberta Street Fair

NE Alberta Street between 10th - 30th Avenues
Portland, OR
www.albertamainst.org/whats-happening/street-fair/
                                        (503) 683-3252

The 18th Annual Alberta Street Fair, features an eclectic mix of sights, sounds and tasty treats that can only be found on Alberta Street.

The fair kicks off with the Annual Kid's Parade and the fun continues all day at the Kid's Corner. The Alberta Street Fair hosts two beer gardens pouring local brews and ciders and that's not all!

Highlights Include:
~ Dancing and music at three stages!
~Unique products & crafts from Alberta's local businesses with 300 vendors!
~Food and beverages from Alberta's well-known eateries, food carts and special vendors!

Admission: Suggested Donation
Kid Friendly Event
Hours: Saturday, August 8 - 11AM - 6PM

Vendor Contact: Kimberly Pillon
streetfairvendor@albertamainst.org
Deadline: 7/24/15
# of Vendors: 300   Not a Juried Event
Attendance: 25,000   # of Years Held: 18

8/8/2015 - 8/9/2015
Detroit Lake Street Festival
Downtown - Detroit Lake, OR
www.centraloregonshows.com   (541) 420-0279

The popular Detroit Lake resort area attracts thousands of visitors each year. This new event offers a variety of arts, crafts, antiques, food, entertainment and a special fundraiser benefiting the Veterans.

Admission: Not Provided
Kid Friendly Event

Vendor Contact: Richard Esterman
centraloregonshows@gmail.com
# of Vendors: 60   Juried Event
# of Years Held: New

8/8/2015 - 8/8/2015
International Praise Fest
Pioneer Courthouse Square - Downtown - Portland, OR

This city-wide event features Christian music performances, praise, dance and kid's activities. Come celebrate God at the International Praise Fest!

Free Admission
Hours: 11am - 6pm

Carnivals, fairs and festivals, oh my,
With cotton candy and rides to the sky!
Animals galore and dunk tanks too,
Fun for the family and fun for you!
~~Catherine Pittman © 2015

8/8/2015 - 8/8/2015
Old Aurora Colony Days
Old Aurora Colony Museum 15018 2nd St.NE Aurora OR
97002 - Aurora, OR
www.auroracolonydays.com   (503) 678-5754

OLD AURORA COLONY DAYS, AUGUST 8, 2015. Old of
the oldest community parades in Oregon's 60+ years of
family fun! Antique and vintage street fair. 4th annual 5K
walk/run & 1k fun run for kids. Parade with floats, classic
cars, bands, horses, equestrian teams, and local
participants. Summer concerts in Aurora Park. Old
Aurora Colony Museum free admission day, and hands-
on pioneer activities. Aurora Art Association art show.

Free Admission
Kid Friendly Event
Hours: Saturday 8 am to 4 pm

Vendor Contact: Noelle Brooks mnoelleb@gmail.com
Deadline: 7/20/15   # of Vendors: 100
Attendance: 1000   # of Years Held: 60

8/8/2015 - 8/8/2015
**Second Saturday at WAAAM Air
& Auto Museum**
1600 Air Museum Road
Hood River, OR
www.waaamuseum.org   541-308-1600

The Second Saturday of each month the WAAAM Air and
Auto Museum opens the doors to roll out and run some
of its antique airplanes and cars. Visitors watch airplane
operations up close and may get to ride in old cars too.
Open 9-5. Activities 10-2. Lunch 11-1. Free parking.
WAAAM is located three miles from downtown Hood
River at 1600 Air Museum Road, Hood River, OR 97031.

Paid Admission
Kid Friendly Event
Hours: Daily 9am-5pm

8/8/2015 - 8/8/2015
Taft Beach Sandcastle Contest
Historic Taft Discrit in Lincoln City - Lincoln City, OR
www.oregoncoast.org

Admission: Not Provided
Kid Friendly Event

Vendor Contact: Historic Taft District

8/10/2015 - 8/13/2015
PDX Young Writers Camp for Kids Entering Grades 6 & 7
Spark Arts Center, 1805 NE Cesar Chavez Blvd
Portland, OR
www.sparkartscenter.com   (503) 281-6757

Youth with a passion for writing are invited to express themselves and share their talents this summer at an exciting new camp. PDX Young Writers Camp will encourage young writers to experiment with different literary genres such as stories, poems, and exploratory essays. The camp will emphasize student voice and student choice; encouraging youth to explore topics that inspire them to write. Experienced instructors and guest authors will challenge students to develop their writing abilities through playful, expressive writing exercises. Artists from Spark Arts Center will lead creative art projects that bring their words to life.

Each day participants will receive individual feedback from an instructor and participate in peer feedback circles. As a culminating celebration, families will be invited to hear students share at least one revised and polished piece. Participants will also go home with a portfolio of work in progress and ideas for continued writing all year long.

Paid Admission
Kid Friendly Event
Hours: Monday - Thursday, 1pm - 4pm

8/11/2015 - 8/15/2015
Umatilla County Fair
Umatilla County Grounds - Hermiston, OR
www.umatillacounty.net/fair/   (541) 567-6121

Admission: Not Provided
Kid Friendly Event

Vendor Contact: Peggy Anderson

8/13/2015 - 8/16/2015
Klamath County Fair
Klamath County Fairgrounds - Klamath Falls, OR
www.kcfairgrounds.org   (541) 883-3796

Paid Admission
Kid Friendly Event

Vendor Contact: Richard "Todd" Hoggarth
kcfg@kcfair.us   # of Vendors: 110
Attendance: 50,000

8/13/2015 - 8/16/2015
North American Organic Brewers Festival
Overlook Park - Portland, OR
www.naobf.org   (503) 296-2779

Two of Portland's beloved industries... organic beer and sustainability come together ine one big annual celebration. Featuring organic beer, cider, braggot and mead along with live music, food, sustainability-oriented vendors, kids area... all in a beautiful park overlooking Portland!

Paid Admission
Kid Friendly Event

Vendor Contact: Chris Crabb chris@naobf.org
# of Years Held: 11

8/13/2015 - 8/15/2015
Quilt! Knit! Stitch!
Oregon Convention Center - Portland, OR
www.quilts.com   (713) 781-6884

One central marketplace for quilt shops and their suppliers. All major fabric, batting, publishing, stencil and pattern companies are represented at this event.

Paid Admission

Vendor Contact: shows@quilts.com
Attendance: 20,000

8/13/2015 - 8/16/2015
Wasco County Fair & Rodeo
81849 Fairgrounds Road - Tygh Valley, OR
www.WascoCounty.Org   541-483-2288

Down home country fair, 4-H, FFA, contests, livestock, horse shows, Carnival, Rodeo 's & Demolition Derby. Bands, Entertainment, Beer Garden. Fun for the whole family!

RV and tent camping available. This is an Oregon Heritage Event.

Paid Admission
Kid Friendly Event
Hours: See Website

Vendor Contact: Kay Tenold kktenold@hotmail.com
Deadline: 8/10/15
# of Vendors: 50   Not a Juried Event
Attendance: 10000   # of Years Held: 100

8/13/2015 - 8/16/2015
Waso County Fair
Wasco County Fairgrounds - Tygh Valley, OR
www.co.wasco.or.us   (541) 483-2288

Paid Admission
Kid Friendly Event

8/13/2015 - 8/16/2015
Zimfest 2015
Western Oregon University
Monmouth, OR
https://2015.zimfest.org
(206) 328-4011

The 24th annual Zimbabwean Music Festival happens at WOU August 13-16, 2015. This "everyone-can-participate" festival offers numerous workshops on Zimbabwean music and culture, free afternoon concerts, continuing education clock hours for teachers, an African marketplace and ticketed evening concerts.

Zimfest 2015 kicks off with the free Opening Ceremony @7:30 p.m. August 13; afternoon concerts and the marketplace open 10 a.m. to 5 p.m. August 14-16.

Visit www.2015.zimfest.org for workshop schedules, registration, concert lineup and tickets.

Free Admission
Kid Friendly Event
Hours: 10 a.m. to 5 p.m.
          Evening concerts F-Sun 7:30 p.m. to 12:00 a.m.

# of Years Held: 23

8/14/2015 - 8/16/2015
Bi-Mart Willamette Country Music Festival
Downtown - Brownsville, OR
www.willamettecountrymusicfestival.com
(541) 345-9263

Admission: Not Provided

Vendor Contact:
info@willamettecountrymusicfestival.com

8/14/2015 - 8/16/2015
Muddy Frogwater Country Classic Festival
Yantis Park, 200 DeHaven St - Milton-Freewater, OR
www.mfchamber.com   541-938-5563

Featuring:
~ a Salmon Bake & Corn Roast
~ Talent of the Valley Competition
~ BBQ Competition
~ Pretty Baby Contest
~ Art Show
~ Kid Zone
~ Vendors
~ Games
~ Free Friday & Saturday Night Concerts.

Free Admission
Kid Friendly Event
Hours: Friday 7am -10pm
            Saturday 7am - 10pm
            Sunday 9am - 4pm

Vendor Contact: Cheryl York
mfmdfrog@mfchamber.com
Not a Juried Event

# of Years Held: 35

2015

Sandy Oktoberfest

FRI., SAT. & SUN.
SEPT. 11-13, 2015

18090 SE Langensand Rd.
Sandy, Oregon

www.sandyoktoberfest.net

8/14/2015 - 8/16/2015
WOE Heritage Fair
2000 N Douglas Dr - Cottage Grove, OR
www.woeheritagefair.com   (541) 942-6150

Pet parade, exhibits, barn animals and an old time
callope!

Admission: Not Provided
Kid Friendly Event

Vendor Contact: Dena Twite   # of Years Held: 83

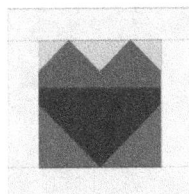

8/15/2015 - 8/16/2015
Heart of the Basin Quilt Show
815 High Street Sacred Heart Gym &
Parrish Hall - Klamath Falls, OR
www.heartofthebasin.com
(541) 892-1354

Quilting Around the Basin Quilt Show sponsored by Heart
of the Basin Quilt Guild in Klamath Falls, Oregon.

Show features traditional & art quilts from around the
Klamath Basin. Displaying over 100 quilts. Vendors, door
prizes, raffle quilt, featured quilter Kirsten Potter, raffle
baskets, challenge quilts and food vendor on site.

Sacred Heart Church gym & parish hall at the corner of
8th and High Streets. See www.heartofthebasin.com for
more details.

Paid Admission
Hours: Saturday 10am - 5pm
          Sunday 10am - 3pm

8/15/2015 - 8/16/2015
Multnomah Day's Street Fair
Multnomah Village: SW 35th Ave & Capitol Hwy
Portland, OR
www.multnomahvillage.org

Free Admission
Kid Friendly Event
Hours: 9am - 10pm

Vendor Contact: Mike Radakovich
mikeradakovich@comcast.net

8/15/2015 - 8/15/2015
Portland Pancakes & Booze Art Show
Hawthorne Theatre - Portland, OR
www.pancakesandbooze.com

Free all-u-can eat pancakes, 50 - 150 local artisan
displays, live music, live canvas and body painting
performances and more!

Admission: Not Provided
No Kid's Activities
Hours: 8pm - 2am

Vendor Contact: pancakesandbooze@gmail.com
# of Vendors: 50

8/15/2015 - 8/16/2015
Silverton Fine Arts Festival
Coolidge-McClaine City Park - Silverton, OR
www.silvertonarts.org   (503) 873-2480

Free Admission
Kid Friendly Event
Hours: Sat: 10am-7pm; Sun: 10am-6pm

Vendor Contact: info@silvertonarts.org
# of Vendors: 85   Juried Event
Attendance: 10000   # of Years Held: 15

8/15/2015 - 8/15/2015
Starlight Express
McEwen Depot - Baker City, OR
www.sumptervalleyrailroad.org

As darkness falls, passengers are treated to a twilight trip up the valley. Complimentary cake and coffee dessert served at the Sumpter station.

Return trip under the stars features the added bonus of the apex of the Perseid Meteor showers, one of the most spectacular events featured on the cosmic calendar!

Paid Admission
Kid Friendly Event
Hours: Leaves 8:00 pm

Vendor Contact: info@sumptervalleyrailroad.org

8/16/2015 - 8/16/2015
Family-Friendly Paddle
Tualatin Community park - Tualatin, OR
www.eventbrite.com/o/tualatin-riverkeepers-
3912079195?s=24161027   (503) 218-2580

You and your family will enjoy a relaxing paddle on the Tualatin River with Tualatin Riverkeepers. No experience necessary, but you are required to print and bring the waiver form.

Space is limited and reservations are required. Personal floatation devices must be worn on the paddle trip.

Paid Admission
Kid Friendly Event

RICE NW MUSEUM OF ROCKS
& MINERALS PRESENTS

TWELFTH ANNUAL

2015 Summer Festival

SAT, AUGUST 1ST ~ SUN, AUGUST 2ND
10:00AM ~ 5:00PM

FEATURING:
MINERAL, FOSSIL, JEWELRY, & BEAD
VENDORS
GOLD PANNING
LAPIDARY DEMONSTRATIONS
GEODE CUTTING
SILENT AUCTIONS, DOOR PRIZES,
& RAFFLES
KIDS' ACTIVITIES
LOCAL FOOD & LIVE MUSIC

**ALSO FEATURING
THE FLINTSTONE MOBILE!**

 Smithsonian Affiliate

ADMISSION
$5 FOR ADULTS
FREE FOR STUDENTS
(17 YEARS OLD AND UNDER)

26385 NW GROVELAND DRIVE
HILLSBORO, OR 97124

WWW.RICENORTHWESTMUSEUM.ORG
503.647.2418

8/16/2015 - 8/16/2015
Hawthorne Street Fair
SE Hawthorne - Portland, OR
www.hathornepdx.com

Free Admission
Hours: 11am - 7pm

Vendor Contact: Nancy Chapin
explore@thinkhawthorne.com

8/17/2015 - 8/19/2015
Beach Blast Camp for Ages 5 1/2 - 10
Spark Arts Cenrer, 1805 NE Cesar Chavez Blvd,
Portland, OR 97212 - Portland, OR
www.sparkartscenter.com   (503) 281-6757

Don't let the sun go down on your summer vacation!
Catch the last bright days of break and transform them
into tie dye shirts, sun catchers, sand painting and more!

Paid Admission
Kid Friendly Event
Hours: M- 12:30-4:30W

8/18/2015 - 8/23/2015
Clackamas County Fair
Clackamas County Fairgrounds - Canby, OR
www.clackamascountyeventcenter.com
(503) 266-1136

Paid Admission
Kid Friendly Event

Vendor Contact: Laurie Bothwell
ccfair@wavecable.com   # of Vendors: 160
Attendance: 125000   # of Years Held: 109

8/18/2015 - 8/25/2015
Concerts in the Park - McCoy
McCoy Park - N Fiske & Trenton - Portland, OR

Free Admission
Hours: Tuesdays - 6:30 pm

8/18/2015 - 8/23/2015
Morrow County Fair & Oregon Trail Pro Rodeo
Morrow County Fairgrounds - Heppner, OR
www.morrowcountyoregon.com/county-fair/
(541) 676-9474

Paid Admission
Kid Friendly Event

Vendor Contact: mcfair@co.morrow.or.us
# of Vendors: 25   Attendance: 3500
# of Years Held: 102

Fun in the Portland Fountain
© *Malia Autio – All Free Downloads*

8/19/2015 - 8/22/2015
Josephine County Fair –
"Carnival Lights & Country Nights"
Josephine County Fairgrounds -- 1451 Fairgrounds Rd
Grants Pass, OR
www.josephinecountyfairgounds.com
(541) 476-3215

2015 Josephine County Fair, Carnival Lights & Country
Nights

Daily Attractions: Sea Lions Splash ~ OMSI ~ 4-H, FFA,
and Open Class Animals & Exhibits ~ Paul Maurer
Carnival

Wednesday, August 19: McCaslin Rodeo -- Grandstands
Thursday, August 20: Knights of the Realm-- Covered
Arena Jousting, Mounted Archers, and Hand-to-Hand
Renaissance Combat

Friday & Saturday August 21 & 22 WGAS Motorsports:
Monster Trucks Open and Street Class Tuff Trucks
Monster Ride Truck & Mud Racing

Admission: Not Provided
Kid Friendly Event
Hours: Wednesday & Thursday - 10a.m. - 10p.m.
Friday & Saturday - 10a.m. - 11p.m.

# of Years Held: 101

8/19/2015 - 8/23/2015
Sherman County Fair
Sherman County Fairgrounds - Moro, OR
www.sherman-county.com   (541) 565-3510

Paid Admission
Kid Friendly Event
Vendor Contact: shermanctyfair@hotmail.com
# of Vendors: 25   Attendance: 10000
# of Years Held: 106

8/21/2015 - 8/23/2015
Art Far & Farmers Market 2015
Ocean's Edge Wayside - Rockaway Beach, OR
www.rockawaybeach.net   (855) 233-6362

Face painting, exquisite handmade arts and crafts, fresh
farm fare and more!

Admission: Not Provided
Kid Friendly Event

Vendor Contact: rbccsec@gmail.com
# of Vendors: 100   # of Years Held: 38

8/21/2015 - 8/23/2015
Northwest Art & Air Festival
Timber Linn Park - Albany, OR
www.nwartandair.org   (541) 917-7777

There is something for everyone in the family at this
one-of-a-kind weekend!   Balloons, night glow, main
stage entertainment, artisan vendors, food, kids area
and more!

Paid Admission
Kid Friendly Event

Vendor Contact: Lynne Jamison
lynne.jamison@cityofalbany.net
# of Vendors: 70   Juried Event
Attendance: 50000   # of Years Held: 16

Listen baby to the music of the night.
Hear the little cricket sing with all her might!
She will play her tiny strings, a sweet lullaby she brings,
As you slumber she will play 'til morn's first light!
~~ Lyrics, A Summer Lullaby by Catherine Pittman from The
Dream Faerie Album © 2000

8/21/2015 - 8/22/2015
Shakespeare in the Park
Drake Park - Bend, OR
www.shakespearebend.com

This event is one of the benchmark cultural events in
Central Oregon. We're bringing back the Bard to Bend
and Sunriver for three brilliant performances of
Shakespeare's quintessential commedy, The Comedy of
Errors.

Paid Admission

Vendor Contact: Emily Arredondo
info@layitoutevents.com

8/22/2015 - 8/22/2015
Kids Obstacle Challenge
Deschutes County Fairgrounds - Bend, OR
www.kidsobstaclechallenge.com

All participating kids will receive a custom dated military
dog tag award to commemorate their accomplishments
on the obstical course, plus goodies our sponsor have to
offer! Prents are free to run alongside their children.

Paid Admission
Kid Friendly Event
Hours: 10am - 1pm; Check-in Opens at 9:30 am

Vendor Contact: eight18productions@gmail.com

Every time I see a rainbow, I find a friend beneath its bright
glow. Together we watch with wondrous eyes, the wee
leprechaun paint and color the skies! So whenever a storm
passes you, look for the rainbow and leprechauns too! And if
you should stand 'neath its light with a friend, then you've
found the gold at the reainbow's end!
~~ Lyrics The Pot of Gold by Catherine Pittman © 1994 from
the Album Topsy Toddler Time

8/22/2015 - 8/23/2015
Sisters Wild West Show
Sisters Creekside Park - Sisters, OR
www.centraloregonshows.com   (541) 420-0279

Plenty of arts and crafts, antiques, food vendors and live
entertainment with a western front town.

Admission: Not Provided
Kid Friendly Event

Vendor Contact: Richard Esterman
centraloregonshows@gmail.com
Juried Event   Attendance: 10000
# of Years Held: 3

8/23/2015 - 8/23/2015
Oregon City Open Air Antique Fair
Main Street - One block off Hwy 99E - Oreon City, OR
www.oregoncity.org   (503) 656-1619

Admission: Not Provided

Vendor Contact: chamberinfo@oregoncity.org
# of Vendors: 87   Attendance: 7000
# of Years Held: 20

8/27/2015 - 8/29/2015
Canyonville Pioneer Days
Canyonville, OR
 (541) 218-2185

Admission: Not Provided
Kid Friendly Event

Vendor Contact: Tamara Hoff   # of Vendors: 90
Attendance: 5000

8/27/2015 - 8/30/2015
Curry County Fair
Curry County Fairgrounds - Gold Beach, OR
www.curryfair.com   (541) 247-4541

Paid Admission
Kid Friendly Event

Vendor Contact: Ron Crook curryfair@gmail.com
# of Vendors: 66   Attendance: 10000

8/27/2015 - 8/29/2015
Festa Italiana Portland
Pioneer Courthouse Square
Portland, OR
www.festa-italiana.org

Celebrating Italian Culture with friends and family in
"Portland's Piazza" Pioneer Courthouse Square. Italian
entertainment, a little opera, ballet, dancing, restaurants
and wine/beer gardens.

This is a family event! Children love face painting, our
puppet theatre, pizza toss and grape stomp.

The event is Free with plenty of transportation to this
downtown location. Raffle- airfare for 2 to Rome, Italian
Scooter and more! See you there

Free Admission
Kid Friendly Event
Hours: Thursday, Friday, Saturday 11am-11pm

# of Years Held: 24th annual

8/28/2015 - 8/30/2015
Art in the High Desert
Downtown Bend - Bend, OR
www.artinthehighdesert.com   (541) 322-6272

Admission: Not Provided
Hours: Fri-Sat: 10am-6pm; Sun: 10am-4pm

Vendor Contact: info@artinthehighdesert.com
Deadline: 2/27/15   # of Vendors: 100+
Juried Event   # of Years Held: 8

8/28/2015 - 9/7/2015
Oregon State Fair
Oregon State Fairgrounds - Salem, OR
www.oregonstatefair.com   (503) 947-3247

Come celebrate our 150th year with over 9,000 things to
eat, drink and enjoy!

Ten outstanding concerts, gourmet cuisine, Oregon
wines, dancing, carnival fun, Familyville, garden stage,
classic cars, blues, brews and BBQ, dogtown, wine patio,
animals, artists village and more!

Paid Admission
Kid Friendly Event

Vendor Contact: Mike Paluszak
osfleadership@oregonstatefair.org
# of Vendors: 620
Attendance: 250,000
# of Years Held: 150

8/29/2015 - 8/29/2015
Aumsville Corn Festival & Parade
Porter-Boone Park - Aumsville, OR
www.aumsville.us   (503) 313-2315

Schedule of events:
11:00 AM
 -Parade
 -Corn Festival in Porter-Boone Park
 -Corn for purchase
12:00PM – 6:00 Pm
 -Hot buttered corn on the cob FREE
 -Live entertainment
 -Food and Crafts vendors
 -Raffle drawing every hour – tickets available from City
 Hall and Riverview Community Bank
1:00 Pm – 5:30 PM Family Games
 -Treasure Hunt
 -3-Legged Race
 -Individual Sack Race
 -Egg Toss
 - Corn Eating Contest
 -Keg Toss
Festival Volunteers – Call 503.313.2325
Parade Volunteers – Call 503.747.1049

Admission: Not Provided
Kid Friendly Event
Hours: 11am - 5:30 pm

Vendor Contact: ltcsonny@gmail.com
# of Vendors: 50
Attendance: 12,000
# of Years Held: 48

8/29/2015 - 8/29/2015
Portland Reptile Expo
Holiday Inn - 8439 NE Columbia Blvd - Portland, OR
www.nwreptileexpos.com

Paid Admission
Kid Friendly Event
Hours: 10am - 5pm

Vendor Contact: reptileexpo@ymail.com

8/29/2015 - 8/30/2015
The Central Oregon Wild West Show
Deschutes County Fairgrounds - Redmond, OR
www.centraloregonshows.com   (541) 420-0279

Paid Admission
Kid Friendly Event

Vendor Contact: Richard Esterman
centraloregonshows@gmail.com
Attendance: 10,000   # of Years Held: 2

8/29/2015 - 8/30/2015
Tillamook Art on the Green
Blue Heron - Adjacent to Hwy 101 - Tillamook, OR
www.centraloregonshows.com   (541) 420-0279

Admission: Not Provided
Kid Friendly Event
Hours: Sat: 10am-5pm;
          Sun: 10am-4pm

Vendor Contact: Richard Esterman
centraloregonshows@gmail.com
# of Years Held: NEW

8/30/2015 - 8/30/2015
20th Oregon City Open Air Antique Fair
Downtown Oregon City - 10th & Main - Oregon City, OR
www.facebook.com/OregonCityOpenAirAntiqueFair
(503) 656-1619

Oregon City's 20th Open Air Antique Fair!

Each year we have more than 80 Antiques and Collectibles booths, as well as music, food vendors and great local businesses.

Discover treasures from yesteryear and perhaps take home something that is just right for your home or the collector in your family. We will also have a "for fun" antique appraiser throughout the day. Come explore historic Downtown Oregon City with us on Sunday, August 30!

Free Admission
No Kid's Activities
Hours: Sunday, August 30, 2015 8:00 am - 4:00 pm

Vendor Contact: Oregon City Chamber of Commerce
chamberinfo@oregoncity.org
Deadline: 8/15/15   # of Vendors: 100
Not a Juried Event
Attendance: 6500   # of Years Held: 20

9/3/2015 - 9/6/2015
Gilliam County Fair
Gilliam County Fairgrounds - Condon, OR
www.co.gilliam.or.us   (541) 384-4139

Paid Admission
Kid Friendly Event

Vendor Contact: Frank Bettencourt fair@co.gilliam.or.us
# of Vendors: 55   Attendance: 2000

September 2015

9/3/2015 - 9/6/2015
Lake County Fair
Lake County Fairgrounds - Lakeview, OR
www.lakecountyor.org   (541) 947-2925

Paid Admission
Kid Friendly Event

Vendor Contact: LeAnne Rogers
lakecofair@yahoo.com
# of Vendors: 50   Attendance: 20000
# of Years Held: 96

9/4/2015 - 9/6/2015
Faerieworlds
Hornings Hideout - North Plains, OR
www.faerieworlds.com

The premiere mystic music and arts festival on the West
Coast!

Featuring bands and musicians from around the world,
and the amazing Mythic Marketplace with over 150
vendors.

Admission: Not Provided

Vendor Contact: vending@faerieworlds.com
Deadline: 8/17/15   # of Vendors: 150

9/4/2015 - 9/4/2015
Sandy Main Street Fall First Friday
Downtown Main Street - Sandy, OR
www.sandymainstreet.org   (503) 489-2173

Come enjoy an evening of dining, art, wine and beer tastings, store specials, live music and more!

Free Admission
Kid Friendly Event
Hours: 5pm - 8pm

Vendor Contact: Jennifer Marks jmarks@ci.sandy.or.us

9/4/2015 - 9/5/2015
The Little Woody Barrel Aged
Brew & Whiskey Festival
Deschutes Historical Center - Bend, OR
www.woodybeer.com   (541) 323-0964

The Little Woody celebrates ancient brewing techniques and is the festival for beer lovers and connoisseurs alike!

Admission: Not Provided

Vendor Contact: Emily Arredondo
info@layitoutevents.com

Deserted Boat Summertime on Whidbey Island
Catherine Pittman © 2013

9/5/2015 - 9/7/2015
Art in the Pearl Fine Arts & Crafts Festival
Pearl District's North Park Blocks - Portland, OR
www.artinthepearl.com   (503) 722-9017

Considered one of the nation's premier art festivals, the Art in the Pearl features jury-selected works from 130 artists from across the USA and Canada. Features exceptional artisans, live music, artist demos, children's art area and a variety of culinary arts.

Admission: Not Provided

Vendor Contact: info@artinthepearl.com
Deadline: 2/28/15   # of Vendors: 130
Juried Event
Attendance: 75000   # of Years Held: 19

9/5/2015 - 9/6/2015
Fort Umpqua Days
Elkton Community Education Center - Elkton, OR
www.elktonbutterflies.com
541 584-2692

A 2 day celebration of Elkton history featuring the ECEC reconstruction of Fort Umpqua, a fur trading post from the 1830s. Includes a bass tournament, parade, vendor & craft booths, historic activities for families, musical history pageant, butterfly flight room, native plant park, food and music both days.

Free Admission
Hours: Saturday & Sunday 9-5

Vendor Contact: Margo Johnson
info@elktonbutterflies.com
Deadline: 8/20/15   # of Vendors: 35
Not a Juried Event   Attendance: 300-40 0/day
# of Years Held: 10

www.juniperjam.com

9/5/2015 - 9/5/2015
Juniper Jam
Wallowa County Fairgrounds - Enterprise, OR

(541) 426-3390

7th annual JUNIPER JAM - The sweetest little music festival in Eastern Oregon! Saturday, September 5, 2015, Labor Day Weekend. Held at the Wallowa County Fairgrounds in the little Eastern Oregon town of Enterprise, this is a great day of music, art, food, drink, and fun for kids.

Gates open at noon, music goes from noon until around 10:00 PM. Tickets are $15 advanced/ $18 at gate, kids 12 & under free. FREE CAMPING!

Paid Admission
Kid Friendly Event
Hours: Saturday, noon-10pm

# of Years Held: 7

©*Harney County Fair – Used With Permission*

9/8/2015 - 9/13/2015

Harney County Fair, Rodeo, & Racemeet
Harney County Fairgrounds - Burns, OR
A new Web page is in progress
(541) 573-6447

The 91st Harney County Fair, Rodeo, and Racemeet will be held at the Harney County Fairgrounds in Burns, Oregon on the dates of September 8-13, 2015. This is truly one of the last "Country Fairs" that will have a multitude of things for a visitor to do. Horse, Racing, Rodeos, Carnival, Vendor Exhibits, Open Class Exhibits, Stage Entertainment, 4H & FFA Youth Livestock Shows & Exhibits, a Parade, a Buckaroo Breakfast, and much, much more!

Paid Admission
Kid Friendly Event
Hours: Daylight until after dark September 8-13, 2015

Vendor Contact: Don Slone hcfair1@centurytel.net
Attendance: 18,000   # of Years Held: 91

Autumn Still Life © David Wagner

9/9/2015 - 9/9/2015
Home School Day
Oregon Garden - Silverton, OR
www.oregongarden.org
(877) 674-2733 or (503) 874-8100

Do you homeschool your child? The Oregon Garden invites 5 - 12 year old home school students to a fun, educational day! Great way to teach your child about the natural world, and get inspired with fun science and art activities! Pre-registration not required.

Admission: Not Provided
Kid Friendly Event
Hours: 10am - 2pm

Vendor Contact: info@oregongarden.org

9/10/2015 - 9/10/2015
The Standard's 2015 Volunteer Expo
Pioneer Courthouse Square - Downtown - Portland, OR
www.standard.com/volunteerexpo

Connect with hundreds of local non-profit organizations to learn how you and your family can volunteer!

Free Admission
Hours: 11am - 2pm

9/10/2015 - 9/13/2015
Wheels & Waves Car Show
Seaside Civic & Convention Center - Seaside, OR
www.flashbackinseaside.com   (503) 738-8585

This annual show benefits the volunteer fire department. Features the Fireman's Casino & Dance and lots of cars!

Paid Admission

9/11/2015 - 9/13/2015
Hells Canyon Mule Days
Wallowa County Fairgrounds - Enterprise, OR
www.hellscanyonmuledays.com   (541) 263-0104

Packed full of mule related happenings with something to
see and do for the whole family!

Admission: Not Provided
Kid Friendly Event

Vendor Contact:
president@hellscanyonmuledays.com
Deadline: 8/15/15   # of Vendors: 35
# of Years Held: 35

---

*Autumn is a second spring when every leaf is a flower. ~~Albert
Camus, Author 1913 – 1960*

*Fall has always been my favorite season. The time when
everything bursts with its last beauty, as if nature had been
saving up all year for the grand finale.
~~ Lauren DeStefano, Author from her book, Wither*

*Leaves dancing in the wind and the air filled with the scent of
crisp and golden apples. There's a sense of anticipation as
nature performs her last glorious array of colorful art.
~~ Catherine Pittman © 2015*

*...September days are here, with summer's best of wheather,
and autumn's best of cheer. ~~ Helen Hunt Jackson*

Autumn is the hush before winter. ~~ French Proverb

*I am struck by the simplicity of light in the atmosphere in the
autumn, as if the earth absorbed none, and out of this profusion
of dazzling light came the autumnal tints. ~~ Henry David
Thoreau, October 12, 1852*

9/11/2015 - 9/13/2015
Sandy Oktoberfest
18090 SE Langensand Road (1/4
mile off Hwy 26) - Sandy, OR
www.sandyoktoberfest.net
503 816 7304

The SANDY OKTOBERFEST is a family-friendly event that has taken place in the Sandy, Oregon mountain community for 17 years. There is free admission to the grounds while enjoying the 75 food and craft vendors; fine art show; Cruisin' Car Show (Sat. 9/12 only) and Kindergarten for kids of all ages (a slight charge). The biergarten features an array of beer and wines and popular music such as country-western; 50-60's rock 'n' roll; popular and blue-grass. Admisions to the biergarten: $4.00 during the day and $7.00 to $12 in the evening, depending on the band playing. There is fun for everyone in the family!

Free Admission
Kid Friendly Event
Hours: Friday 5:00pm - 11:00pm
          Saturday 11:00am - 11:00pm
          Sunday 10:30am - 4:40pm

Vendor Contact: Sheryl Abraham
sheryl@detailplus.com
Deadline: 7/30/15   # of Vendors: 75
Juried Event
Attendance: 8,000 to 10,000   # of Years Held: 17

9/11/2015 - 9/13/2015
Sisters Folk Festival
The Village Green Park - Sisters, OR
www.sistersfolkfestival.org   (541) 549-4979

Admission: Not Provided

Vendor Contact: info@sistersfolkfestival.com
# of Vendors: 10   Attendance: 4000

9/12/2015 - 9/13/2015
Annual Hood River Fly-In
1600 Air Museum Road
Hood River, OR

www.waaamuseum.org/   541-308-1600

Enjoy hundreds of visiting airplanes, food and activities. See airplanes close at hand and visit with the pilots. Airplane and biplane rides. Acres of free parking.

Come celebrate WAAAM Air and Auto Museum's Birthday. Museum open 9-5. Lions Club breakfast 8 am Sat/Sun.

WAAAM is located three miles from downtown Hood River at 1600 Air Museum Road, Hood River, OR 97031. Call (541) 308-1600 for more information or visit www.waaamuseum.org.

Paid Admission
Kid Friendly Event
Hours: Daily 9am-5pm
         Event Times 8am-5pm both days

# of Years Held: 9

Vintage Bi-plane © Nightowl All Free Downloads

9/12/2015 - 9/12/2015
Carlton Crush Harvest Festival
Upper Park & Downtown Carlton - Carlton, OR
www.carltoncrush.com   (971) 237-1045

The Carlton Crush Harvest Festival, a day-long celebration of the people, businesses and magnificent quality of life in Carlton and Yamhill County. Featuring a Grape Stomp Competition, Barrel Rolling Race, Wine Thief Relay Race, Kids' Watermelon Eating Contest, vintage car display, live music and entertainment, helicopter rides, an Artists' Market, and terrific food from a variety of restaurants.

The Crush Corral features fine wines and craft beers from wineries and breweries throughout the area.

Registration Forms for all competitions are available on the event's website at www.CarltonCrush.com.

Sponsored by the Carlton Business Association

Free Admission
Kid Friendly Event
Hours: 10am - 10pm

Vendor Contact: Terry McIntyre

...September is dressing herself in showy dahlias and splendid marigolds and starry zinnias.
~~Oliver Wendel Holmes, Poet 1809-1894

9/12/2015 - 9/13/2015
Sisters Fall Street Festival
Sisters High School - Sisters, OR
www.centraloregonshows.com   (541) 420-0279

Benefits Sisters High School Visual Arts Department, the
event features arts and crafts, food, entertainment.

Admission: Not Provided

Vendor Contact: Richard Esterman
centraloregonshows@gmail.com
# of Vendors: 85   Juried Event
Attendance: 10000   # of Years Held: 8

9/13/2015 - 9/13/2015
Celebration in Boring
Boring Middle School - Boring , OR
www.celebrationinboring.com

Free Admission
Kid Friendly Event
Hours: 10am - 3pm

# of Vendors: 30+   # of Years Held: 1000+

9/13/2015 - 9/13/2015
Grandparent's Day
McEwen Depot - Baker City, OR
www.sumptervalleyrailroad.org

Family passes just got better! Add two grandparents to
your round trip or one-way family pass for free!

Paid Admission
Kid Friendly Event

Vendor Contact: info@sumptervalleyrailroad.org

9/17/2015 - 9/20/2015
Mount Angel Oktoberfest
Mount Angel OR - Mount Angel , OR
www.oktoberfest.org   (855) 899-6338

In the heart of Oregon, Mount Angel's Oktoberfest brings 350,000 people to the Bavarian village every September. The Northwest's oldest and best loved Folk Festival - celebrates the fruits of the harvest, and the goodness of Creation! There is something for everyone at the Mount Angel Oktoberfest.

Free Admission
Hours: Thurs - Sat 11-10pm Sun 11am-7pm

Vendor Contact: Jeff Cuff thecuff4@mtangel.net
Deadline: 4/30/15   # of Vendors: 120
Juried Event
Attendance: 350000   # of Years Held: 50

9/18/2015 - 9/19/2015
Feast Portland Oregon Bounty Grand Tasting
Pioneer Courthouse Square - Downtown - Portland, OR
www.feastportland.com

Paid Admission
Hours: Begins 9am

Vendor Contact: info@feastportland.com
# of Vendors: 50

9/18/2015 - 9/20/2015
Winston-Dillard Melon Festival
Riverbend Park - Winston, OR   (541) 679-9466

Admission: Not Provided
Kid Friendly Event

Vendor Contact: Ann wdfest@gmail.com
# of Years Held: 47

9/19/2015 - 9/20/2015
22nd Annual Polish Festival
3900 N Failing St - Portland, OR
www.portlandpolonia.org

Free Admission
Kid Friendly Event

9/19/2015 - 9/20/2015
Bay Area Fun Festival
Downtown & Surrounding Area - Coos Bay, OR
www.bayareafunfestival.com

Admission: Not Provided
Kid Friendly Event

Vendor Contact: info@bayareafunfestival.com

9/19/2015 - 9/19/2015
Indian Style Salmon Bake
Depoe Bay City Park - Depoe Bay, OR
www.depoebaychamber.org   (541) 765-2889

Approximately 3000 pounds of salmon are cooked to
perfection on wooden stakes over open fires of alder and
cedar...just as the Indians did it years ago!

Includes a full day of live entertainment.

Admission: Not Provided
Hours: 10am - 5pm

Native American Dance
© Michelle Walters
All Free Downloads

9/19/2015 - 9/19/2015
International Model A Day at
the WAAAM Air & Auto Museum
1600 Air Museum Road - Hood
River, OR

www.waaamuseum.org   (541) 308-1600

Come celebrate Model A Day at the WAAAM Air and Auto
Museum.

Bring your Model A out for a fall drive and share the joy
of antique car ownership with the world. There is nothing
like seeing all of these old cars in motion. WAAAM is
located three miles from downtown Hood River at 1600
Air Museum Road, Hood River, OR 97031. Call (541)
308-1600   for   more   information   or   visit
www.waaamuseum.org

Paid Admission
Kid Friendly Event
Hours: Daily 9am-5pm Event 10am-2pm

9/19/2015 - 9/19/2015
River Clean-up at Tualatin Community Park
Tualatin Community park - Tualatin, OR
www.eventbrite.com/o/tualatin-riverkeepers-
3912079195?s=24161027   (503) 218-2580

Help clean the Tualatin River while enjoying a paddle
trip! Paddlers will pick-up trach along the way. Gloves
and trash receptacles will be provided. Participants must
bring the waiver form and personal floatation devices
work.

Paid Admission
Kid Friendly Event

9/22/2015 - 9/27/2015
Celebration of Honor
Chinook Winds Casino Resort - Lincoln City, OR
www.oregoncoast.org   (541) 996-5766

Free Admission

Vendor Contact: Heather Hatton
heatherh@CWCResort.com

9/24/2015 - 9/27/2015
Oregon's Alpenfest
59919 Wallowa Lake Hwy - Joseph, OR
www.oregonalpenfest.blogspot.com (503) 692-5050

This long-running event is widely known as 'Oregon's Little Switzerland." Features polka music and dancing, yodeling, alphorns, Swiss and German cuisine, beer and wine, arts and crafts, antiques and gift shopping!

Admission: Not Provided
Kid Friendly Event

Vendor Contact: lakesidelynn@eoni.com

9/25/2015 - 9/25/2015
American Indian Day Celebration
Pioneer Courthouse Square - Downtown - Portland, OR

Celebrating our local tribes heritage! Featuring Northwest Tribal leaders, indian advocates, drum groups, dancers, arts and crafts vendors, and more!

Free Admission
Hours: 12pm - 7pm

9/25/2015 - 10/31/2015
Mahaffy Ranch Pumpkin Patch
Mahaffy Ranch - Coos Bay, OR
www.mahaffyranch.com   (541) 269-3900

Mahaffy Ranch invites you to "Make a Day of It" in the
country! Our desire is to provide a family friendly
experience in our beautiful harvest setting. Our
experience here is unique and rustic, come see for
yourself!

Family Friendly U-Pick Pumpkin Patch, Hay Rides, Corn
Maze, Corn Cannons, farm animals, BBQ and more!
School Field Trips and Birthday Parties by appointment
only! Please check our website for scheduled events -
pumpkin chunkin, square dancing, fiddlers, and
workshops!

Free Admission
Kid Friendly Event
Hours: M-F 12-5 Sat & Sun 10-6

# of Years Held: 5

© Oaks Park Association
Oktoberfest at Oaks Park
Amusement Park
Used With Permission

9/25/2015 - 9/27/2015
Paulaner Oktoberfest at Oaks
Amusement Park
Oaks Amusement Park - Portland, OR
www.oakspark.com (503) 233-5777

Portland's Premier fall festival is back with authentic German food and beer, live oompah bands, polka dancing, wiener dog races, cooking demonstrations, local craft and import vendors, Kinderplatz children's area, and much, much more!

Completely family friendly; children welcome all hours in all event venues. Parking free.

Paid Admission
Kid Friendly Event
Hours: Friday: 3:00 PM - 12:00 Midnight Saturday: 11:00 AM - 12:00 Midnight Sunday: 11:00 AM - 7:00 PM

Vendor Contact: Emily MacKay
emckay@oakspark.com
Deadline: 8/30/15   # of Vendors: 30+
Attendance: 25,000   # of Years Held: 20+

Oktoberfest at Oaks Park September 2012 © Oaks Park Association Used With Permision

9/25/2015 - 10/31/2015
Wooden Shoe Pumpkin Fest
33814 S Meridian Rd - Woodburn, OR
www.woodenshoe.com   503-634-2243

This fall bring your family to our family farm and enjoy walking through a pictured corn maze, bouncing through mud in our famous cow trains, breathing in the fresh fall air, and much more.

Pick a pumpkin from our pumpkin patch to take home and see if you can sneak a glimpse of Mt. Hood between rain showers.

Paid Admission
Kid Friendly Event
Hours: Friday - Sunday 10am-6pm

# of Vendors: NA
Attendance: 8000   # of Years Held: 7

9/26/2015 - 11/1/2015
13th Door Haunted House
3855 SW Murray Blvd - Beaverton, OR
www.13thdoor.com   (503) 410-1816

You will experience Portland's best haunted attraction at the 13th Door Haunted House!   Join the oldest Halloween attraction at our 13th anniversary!

Paid Admission
Kid Friendly Event
Hours: See website

Vendor Contact: the13thdoor@hotmail.com
# of Years Held: 13

9/26/2015 - 9/27/2015
Corvallis Fall Festival
Central Park - Corvallis, OR
www.corvallisfallfestival.org   (541) 752-9655

Celebrating our 43rd year! 160+ artisan vendors, 14+ food carts, tasting tables for local wines, beers, ciders and spirits!

Admission: Not Provided
Kid Friendly Event
Hours: Sat: 10am-6pm; Sun: 10am-5pm

Deadline: 5/1/15   # of Vendors: 170   Juried
EventAttendance: 35,000   # of Years Held: 43

9/26/2015 - 9/26/2015
ECEC Oktoberfest
Elkton community Education Center - Elkton, OR
www.elktonbutterflies.com
541 584-2692

Join ECEC for a fall harvest and Oktoberfest celebration on Saturday, September 26 from noon to 4pm. Cover charge and food sales of German foods, served by local service organizations , "beer and brats" served by ECEC. Live music and "polka till you drop" with the Roseburg German Band, on the patio at ECEC, 15850 Hwy 38, Elkton

Paid Admission
Kid Friendly Event
Hours: Noon - 4pm

Attendance: 100+   # of Years Held: 42130

9/26/2015 - 10/30/2015
French Prairie Gardens Pumpkin Patch
French Prairie Gardens & Family Farm - St. Paul, OR
www.fpgardens.com   (503) 633-8445

Admission: Not Provided
Kid Friendly Event
Hours: Tues-Sat: 9am-5pm;
        Sun: 10am-5pm.
        Closed Mondays.

9/26/2015 - 9/26/2015
Hood River Hops Fest
Hood River Event Center - Hood River, OR
www.hoodriver.org/hops-fest   (541) 386-2000

Some of the best of the Northwest brewers will be found
at this event that showcases Hood River County's own
microbreweries.

Admission: Not Provided

Vendor Contact: admin@hoodriver.org
Deadline: 7/1/15
# of Vendors: 100   Juried Event
Attendance: 10000

9/26/2015 - 9/27/2015
Oregon Flock & Fiber Festival
Clackamas County Fairgrounds - Canby, OR
www.facebook.com/pages/Oregon-Flock-and-
Fiber-Festival/198066350228459 (503) 628-1205

Admission: Not Provided
Kid Friendly Event

# of Vendors: 125   Juried Event
Attendance: 8000   # of Years Held: 19

9/26/2015 - 9/27/2015
Pacific City Artist Marketplace
Downtown Sisters - Pacific City, OR
www.centraloregonshows.com   (541) 420-0279

Admission: Not Provided

Vendor Contact: Richard Esterman
centraloregonshows@gmail.com
Juried Event   # of Years Held: NEW

9/28/2015 - 9/28/2015
The Diamonds Bandstand Boogie
Wahtonka High School: 220 E 10th St - The Dalles, OR
www.mccca.info   (541) 506-3400

The Diamonds have discovered the durability of classic rock 'n' roll and their audiences continue to expand at venues around the world!

Admission: Not Provided
Hours: 7pm

Black & White Leaves
© Zdenet
All Free Downloads

October 2015

10/1/2015 - 10/30/2015
Halloween Fantasy Trail Wenzel Farm
19754 So. Ridge Road, Oregon City, OR
www.fantasytrail.com   (503) 631-2047

Take a walk through a lighted, wooded "FANTASY TRAIL'
decorated with spooky sights and sounds at Halloween,
decorated with thousands of lights for your Christmas
enchantment.

Also, walk through 40' castle with Halloween and
Christmas scenes. Have fun on suspension bridge, walk
through tunnel, maze or crooked house! Bonfire nightly
at Christmas. Everything is geared in age from 0 - 100
years. Great for families.

Halloween Fantasy Trail will be celebrating its 21st year
while Christmas Fantasy Trail will be celebrating its 23rd
year.

Paid Admission
Kid Friendly Event
Hours: See website www.fantasytrail.com for days and
hours of operation

# of Years Held: 23 years

October, the extravagant sister, has ordered an immense
amount of the most gorgeous forest tapestry for her grand
reception.
~~Oliver Wendell Holmes, Poet 1809-1894

10/1/2015 - 10/31/2015
Haunted Candelight Tours at the Oregon Caves
On Hwy 46 at 201 - Cave Junction, OR
www.nps.gov

You'll get goose-bumps on this fun toor that includes spooky stories of local history. So come walk among the bats and spiders, and discover the Oregon Caverns in a whole new light!

Admission: Not Provided

10/1/2015 - 10/4/2015
Local 14 Women's Art Show & Sale
World Forestry Center's Miller Hall - Portland, OR
www.local14.org   (503) 650-0046

This annual event represents the artwork of approximately 85 women artists from the Pacific Northwest.

Art is showcased in a gallery setting, often highlighting special themes.

Admission: Not Provided
No Kid's Activities
Hours: Fri: 10am-7pm
            Sat & Sun: 10am-5pm

Vendor Contact: fiberalchemy@comcast.net
Deadline: 3/16/15   Juried Event
# of Years Held: 49

Pixie kobold elf and sprit,
All are on their rounds tonight;
In the wan moon's silver ray,
Thrives their helter-skelter play.
~~Joel Benton, American Writer 1832 - 1911

10/2/2015 - 10/4/2015
Albany Home and Remodel Show
Linn County Fair & Expo Center
Albany, OR

events
www.wvpevents.com

(503) 364-1716

The 2015 Albany Home & Remodel Show is the Home Improvement event for Linn and Benton Counties! For 21 straight years, the AHRS has had an immense impact on the community and enjoys being a city favorite :)

Great prices on booth displays and it's always a highlight for the year for many. 503.364.1716 for more info.

Paid Admission
Hours: Friday: 3-8
        Saturday: 10-8
        Sunday: 10-5

Vendor Contact: Kaleb Ramsay kaleb@wvpevents.com
Deadline: 9/15/15   # of Vendors: 200

10/2/2015 - 10/4/2015
Bend Fall Festival
Downtown Bend - Bend, OR
www.c3events.com

(541) 383-3026

Admission: Not Provided
Kid Friendly Event
Hours: Fri: 5pm-10pm
        Sat: 11am-10pm
        Sun: 11am-5pm

Vendor Contact: artists@c3events.com
Deadline: 9/20/15   Juried Event

10/3/2015 - 10/3/2015
Affordable Art For Everyone
NW Events 2900 NW 229th Ave - Hillsboro, OR
www.affordableartforeveryone.com (503) 318-5227

Affordable Art for Everyone is a special free public buying event with over 70 artists offering high-quality work for under $100.

Juried fine art and crafts include paintings, ceramics, glass, jewelry, wood, metalwork and photography. A unique opportunity to purchase quality art at outstanding prices, AAFE takes place at NW Events in Hillsboro, Oregon, a spacious facility conveniently located 20 minutes west of Portland. AAFE will also offer performing arts activities for the whole family.

Free Admission
Kid Friendly Event
Hours: Saturday October 3 11am to 6pm

Vendor Contact: Debby Garman
debby.creativehillsboro@gmail.com
Deadline: Varies   # of Vendors: 100+
Juried Event   # of Years Held: first year

10/3/2015 - 10/3/2015
Autumn River Paddle
Tualatin Community park - Tualatin, OR
www.eventbrite.com/o/tualatin-riverkeepers-
3912079195?s=24161027   (503) 218-2580

Bring your cameras for this not-to-be-missed brilliant fall colors along the Tualatin River. No experience necessary. Requires waiver form and personal flotation devices must be worn on the trip.

Paid Admission
Kid Friendly Event

10/3/2015 - 10/31/2015
E.Z. Orchards Harvest Festival
E.Z. Orchards Farm Market - Salem, OR
www.ezorchards.com   (503) 393-1506

E.Z. Orchards Annual Harvest Festival boasts fun for all ages! Join us for our u-pick pumpkin patch, corn maze, petting zoo, pony rides, hay rides, pedal tractors, duck races, steer ropin', gold mining, face painting, and live music! Make memories or start a new family tradition at E.Z. Orchards Harvest Festival! Stop by our market while you're here for our famous Apple Cider and Apple Cider doughnuts!

Paid Admission
Kid Friendly Event
Hours: Saturdays 9:00-5:00 Sundays 11:00-5:00

Attendance: Thousands
# of Years Held: 19 Years

10/3/2015 - 10/31/2015
FrightTown
Veterans Memorial Coliseum - Portland, OR
www.frighttown.com   503-97GHOST

FrightTown is Oregon's number one Halloween haunted attraction, with three huge haunted houses and a whole city block of shock! Returning to the Rose Quarter every October, FrightTown features new scares and thrills every time! Be sure to visit www.frighttown.com for more information and show times. Please note that FrightTown is too intense and scary for young children.

Paid Admission
Too Scary and intense for young children
Hours: Friday & Saturday 7pm-11pm Wednesday, Thursday, Sunday 7pm-10pm
Closed Mondays and Tuesdays

Attendance: 40000   # of Years Held: 11

10/3/2015 - 10/3/2015
Wild Mushroom Cook-off
Cullinary Center - 801 SW Hwy 101 - Lincoln City, OR
www.oregoncoast.org   (541) 996-1273

Live presentations, wild mushroom identification, food vendors, wild mushroom books, wild mushrooms for sale and more!

Free Admission
Hours: 11am - 2pm

Vendor Contact: Suzanne Treece

10/6/2015 - 10/8/2015
Portland Artisan Market - Fall Market
Pioneer Courthouse Square - Downtown - Portland, OR

Our annual fall market features creative artisans selling their handmade wares. Includes woodworkers, jewelry, art, photography, and more.

Free Admission
# of Vendors: 40

10/7/2015 - 10/29/2015
The Haunted Ghost Town
Rossi Farms - 3839 NE 122nd Ave - Portland, OR
(971) 266-1781

Admission: Not Provided
Kid Friendly Event
Hours: Fridays & Saturdays: 7pm - 10pm;
           Sundays:7pm - 9:30 pm

Halloween...
Where Ghoules, Ghosts & Goblins come creeping to your door,
Hoping to scare you for a treat and a whole lot more!
~~Catherine Pittman © 2015

10/9/2015 - 10/11/2015
33rd Lane County Home Improvement Show
Lane Co. Convention Center - Fairgrounds - Eugene, OR
www.EugeneHomeshow.com   (541) 484-9247

Showcasing Great Home & Garden Transformations!
Shop & compare 250 exhibits featuring experts, products
and services for homes & yards. Learn "How-to"
at 50 seminars.   FREE admission with canned food
donations.   FREE Parking. Fri: 5pm-9pm, Sat: 10am-
8pm, Sun: 10am-5pm.   www.EugeneHomeShow.com

Free Admission with canned food donations
No Kid's Activities
Hours: Fri: 5pm-9pm
          Sat: 10am-8pm
          Sun: 10am-5pm.

Vendor Contact: Beth Little
info@eugenehomeshow.com
Deadline: When Filled   # of Vendors: 360
Juried Event   # of Years Held: 33

10/10/2015 - 10/11/2015
Fall Festival & Pumpkin Patch
St. Frederick Catholic Church - St. Helens, OR

Admission: Not Provided

Vendor Contact: stfred@comcast.net
# of Vendors: 25   Not a Juried Event
Attendance: 1500   # of Years Held: 3

10/10/2015 - 10/10/2015
Great Onion Festival
Archer Glen Elementary School - 16155 SW Sunset Blvd
Sherwood, OR

Free Admission

10/10/2015 - 10/10/2015
Haines Harvest Festival
925 3rd St - Haines, OR
http://www.visiteasternoregon.com/entry/haines
-harvest-festival-2/   (541) 519-8887

Enjoy the fall colors and the changing of the seasons while visiting the Haines Harvest Festival. A quintessential small town celebration!

Providing a fun-filled day of kids crafts, games apple cider, arts and crafts vendors and more

Free Admission
Kid Friendly Event

Vendor Contact: lahaugfamily@hotmail.com

10/10/2015 - 10/11/2015
Northwest CiderFest
Pioneer Courthouse Square - Downtown - Portland, OR
www.nwciderfest.org   (503) 223-3177

Paid Admission

# of Vendors: 30

10/10/2015 - 10/10/2015
Portland Pet Expo
Portland Expo Center - Portland, OR
www.portlandpetexpo.com (800) 977-3609 ext. 108

Paid Admission
Kid Friendly Event

Vendor Contact: Kati Keyes
# of Vendors: 120   Attendance: 10000

10/10/2015 - 10/10/2015
Second Saturday at WAAAM Air & Auto Museum
1600 Air Museum Road
Hood River, OR

www.waaamuseum.org   541-308-1600

The Second Saturday of each month the WAAAM Air and Auto Museum opens the doors to roll out and run some of its antique airplanes and cars.

Visitors watch airplane operations up close and may get to ride in old cars too. Open 9-5. Activities 10-2. Lunch 11-1. Free parking.

WAAAM is located three miles from downtown Hood River at 1600 Air Museum Road, Hood River, OR 97031.

Paid Admission
Kid Friendly Event
Hours: Daily 9am-5pm

10/10/2015 - 10/11/2015
Sisters Harvest Faire
Hood Avenue - Sisters, OR   (541) 549-0251

Admission: Not Provided
Hours: 10am - 4pm

Vendor Contact: Jeri Buckmann
jeri@sisterscountry.com   # of Years Held: 34

Bittersweet October. The mellow, messy, leaf-kicking, perfect pause between the opposing miseries of summer and winter.
~~Carol Bishop Hipps, "October," In a Southern Garden 1995

10/15/2015 - 10/18/2015
Oregon State Salem Fall RV Show
Oregon State Fairgrounds - Salem, OR
www.salem.fallrvshow.com   (206) 248-8430

Oregon's Largest RV Show
Paid Admission
No Kid's Activities
Hours: Thursday 10am - 7pm
         Friday 10am - 7pm
         Saturday 10am - 7pm
         Sunday 10am - 5pm

Vendor Contact: Bill Bradley bbwestlake@seanet.com
# of Vendors: N/A
Attendance: 15000   # of Years Held: 36

10/16/2015 - 10/16/2015
Fall Colors Train
McEwen Depot - Baker City, OR
www.sumptervalleyrailroad.org

Paid Admission
Kid Friendly Event
Hours: two trips out of the McEwen Depot: 10am and
1:15; one round trip from the Sumpter depot: Noon

Vendor Contact: info@sumptervalleyrailroad.org

As spirits roam the neighborhoods at night,
Let loose upon the Earth till it be light...
~~ Nicholas Gordon, www.poemsforfree.com

From ghoulies and ghosties and long-leggedy beasties,
And things that go bump in the night,
Good Lord, deliver us!
~~ Scottish Saying

10/16/2015 - 10/18/2015
Hood River Valley Harest Fest
Hood River Event Center - Hood River, OR
www.hoodriver.org   (541) 386-2000

Harvest Fest is a great place to get your head start on holiday shopping! You'll find an array of artisan vendors, kids zone, food court, and more! Visitors seldom leave without boxes of Anjou pears, heirloom apples, and a smorgasbord of handmade pies, jams, smoked salmon, chocolate covered cherries and more!

Admission: Not Provided
Kid Friendly Event
Hours: Fri: 1pm - 7pm;
        Sat: 10am-7pm;
        Sun: 10am-5pm

Vendor Contact: admin@hoodriver.org
Deadline: 5/15/15   # of Vendors: 100   Juried Event
Attendance: 30000   # of Years Held: 33

Halloween Still Life © Jeanette O'Neal

10/16/2015 - 10/18/2015
Portland Christmas Cash & Carry Gift Show
Oregon Convention Center - Portland, OR
www.candcshows.com   (800) 318-2238

The Portland Christmas Cash & Carry Gift Shows will bring retailers a versatile collection of gifts-to-go, just in time to fill inventory gaps for the all important 4th quarter holiday buying season. Featuring the biggest and best selection in the west, buyers will find exactly what they're looking for, with no long wait for delivery---order writing and immediate delivery of merchandise is available. The vast selection includes: Gifts & Collectibles, Fine and Fashion Jewelry, Antiques, Aromatherapy, Bath & Spa Items, Handcrafted Items, Gourmet Food Products, Holiday Merchandise, Personal & Fashion Accessories and More!

Free Admission
Hours: Fri., Oct. 16: 10am- 5 pm
            Sat., Oct. 17: 10 am- 5 pm
            Sun., Oct. 18: 10 am- 4 pm

Vendor Contact: Jim Walker jwalker@urban-expo.com
Not a Juried Event

10/17/2015 - 10/18/2015
Gorge Fruit & Craft Fair
Hood River County Fairgrounds - Hood River, OR
www.hoodriverfair.org   (541) 354-2865

Featuring arts and crafts, gourmet food, fresh fruit and produce, wine, special attractions, carnival rides, garden club flower show, wine tasting and live music.

Admission: Not Provided
Kid Friendly Event
Hours: 10am - 5pm

Vendor Contact: hrfair@hrecn.net   # of Vendors: 90

10/17/2015 - 10/18/2015
Photographer's Weekend
McEwen Depot - Baker City, OR
www.sumptervalleyrailroad.org

This annual event is for fans of history! It's a full day of fun with trains operating over the entire line both Saturday & Sunday.

Enjoy the beautiful fall colors, vintage steam locomotive and a fleet of historic freight and passenger equipment that performs numerous photo stops throughout the day. Breakfast and lunch included. Reservations required.

Paid Admission
Hours: Departs McEwen depot each day at 7am

Vendor Contact: info@sumptervalleyrailroad.org

10/17/2015 - 10/17/2015
Portland DeafNation Expo
Portland Expo Center - Portland, OR
www.deafnation.com/dnexpo/   (775) 314-6337

Jam-packed with activities that is perfect for any age! Learn about cutting-edge technology, products and services while socializing and participating in fun, family-friendly activities.

Paid Admission

October's poplars are flaming torches lighting the way to winter.
~~Nova S Blair, Author

10/17/2015 - 10/17/2015
West Coast Giant Pumpkin Regatta
Lake of the Commons, 8325 SW
Nyberg Street - Tualatin, OR
www.tualatinoregon.gov/recreatio
n/west-coast-giant-pumpkin-
regatta-official-page

503-691-3076

The world famous West Coast Giant Pumpkin Regatta is a series of wacky races around the Lake of Tualatin Commons in 1000 lb. pumpkin boats by costumed participants.

The event also features music, pie eating contests, kids pumpkin carving, face painting, pumpkin golf, pumpkin bowling, a kids costume contest, Smokey and Rojo the Llama Boys, strolling entertainment, inflatable obstacle courses, clown shows, hot food and drinks, and much more!

Free Admission
Kid Friendly Event
Hours: Saturday 10:00am-4:00pm

Attendance: 5000-7000   # of Years Held: 11

10/17/2015 - 10/18/2015
WFF Artisan Craft Fair
Florence Events Center - Florence, OR
www.ci.florence.or.us   (888) 968-4086

Free Admission
Hours: 11am - 5pm

Vendor Contact: wffartisanfair@gmail.com
Deadline: 10/1/15   Juried Event

10/23/2015 - 10/24/2015
Columbia River Gorge Quilt Show
Hood River Armory - 1590 12th St - Hood River, OR
www.gorgequiltersguild.org/quiltshow.html
(405) 747-9353

Admission: Not Provided
Hours: 10am - 5pm

Vendor Contact: vette61@me.com
# of Vendors: 20
Attendance: 1000
# of Years Held: 13

10/23/2015 - Oct. 25, 2015
Salem Home & Remodel Show
Oregon State Fairgrounds - Salem,
OR

www.wvpevents.com   (503) 364-1716

The 26th Salem Home & Remodel Show has a lot in
store for the fun, event this Fall!

Join us in October for the Home Improvement and
Remodeling event for the Mid-Valley Region of the
Willamette Valley. With over 200 companies, the Oregon
State Fairgrounds will be bursting at the seams ... don't
miss the Home Show weekend! 503.364.1716
www.wvpevents.com

Admission: Not Provided
Hours: F: 3-8 S: 10-8 Su: 10-5

Vendor Contact: Kaleb Ramsay kaleb@wvpevents.com
Deadline: 9/15/15
# of Vendors: 230

10/24/2015 - 10/25/2015
All About the Horses
Deschutes County Expo Center - Redmond, OR
www.allaboutthehorses.com   (541) 810-8858

Great entertainment and lots of "horsey" fun including educationel events and seminars, Wild Mustang Competition and more.

Admission: Not Provided

Vendor Contact: Bob & Kori Crutcher
allaboutthehorses1@gmail.com
# of Vendors: 70
Attendance: 5000-10000

10/24/2015 - 10/24/2015
Barn Dance
Oregon Garden - Silverton, OR
www.oregongarden.org
(877) 674-2733 or (503) 874-8100

Yeehaw! Featuring line dancing lessons, pig roast, beer and more!

Paid Admission
Vendor Contact: info@oregongarden.org

10/24/2015 - 10/25/2015
Portland Expo Center Antique & Collectable Show
Portland Expo Center - Portland, OR
www.christinepalmer.net   (503) 282-0877

Paid Admission
# of Vendors: 450

10/25/2015 - 10/25/2015
Run Like Hell!
Pioneer Courthouse Square - Downtown - Portland, OR

Dress up in your Halloween costume and run the kids half mile, 5k, 10k or half marathon through downtown Portland. This is a fun Halloween event for the entire family. Register today.

Paid Admission
Kid Friendly Event
Hours: Begins at 9:00 am

10/26/2015 - 10/26/2015
Talking Tombstones
TBA - Astoria, OR
www.oldoregon.com

Former citizens are expected to return from the great beyond at the annual Talking Tombstones!

Free Admission
Kid Friendly Event
Hours: 1pm - dusk

Vendor Contact: cchs@cumtux.org

10/31/2015 - 10/31/2015
Ashland Chamber Children's Halloween Celebration
Public Library - Ashland, OR
www.ashlandchamber.com

Spend your Halloween safely! This year's children's Halloween includes Halloween Story Time (Ashland Public Library), Parade,

Free Admission
Kid Friendly Event
Hours: Begins at 2:30 pm

November 2015

11/6/2015 - 11/8/2015
5th Annual Columbia Gorge Fiber Festival
Ft. Dalles Readiness Center - The Dalles, OR
www.columbiagorgefiberfestival.com
(541) 308-0002

The 5th annual gathering for fiber enthusiasts in the PNW, featuring a marketplace with 40+ vendors offering everything from hand-dyed yarn to artisan cheese. Workshops and demos for spinning, knitting and weaving.

Parking and admission to the marketplace are free! Festival begins Friday evening at 4:00pm with a Marketplace Kick-Off and No-Host Happy Hour. Marketplace hours continue Saturday and Sunday; keynote banquet Saturday night, and workshops in knitting, spinning, weaving, felting, and more run Friday-Sunday.

Free Admission
Kid Friendly Event
Hours: Friday education all day, market 4-7
        Saturday education all day, market 9-6
        Sunday education AM, market 9-2.

Vendor Contact: Sarah Keller
info@columbiagorgefiberfestival.com
# of Vendors: 40   Juried Event
Attendance: 600+   # of Years Held: 5

11/6/2015 - 11/8/2015
Eugene Gem Faire
Lane County Events Center - Eugene, OR
www.gemfaire.com   (503) 252-8300

Fine jewelry, precious & semi-precious gemstones, millions of beads, crystals, gold & silver, minerals & much more at manufacturer's prices.

Over 70 exhibitors from around the world. Jewelry repair & cleaning while you shop. Free hourly door prizes. For more info, visit www.gemfaire.com or call (503) 252-8300 or email: info@gemfaire.com.

Paid Admission
No Kid's Activities
Hours: Fri Noon-6pm
          Sat 10am-6pm
          Sun 10am-5pm

Vendor Contact: Allen Van Volkinburgh
info@gemfaire.com
Deadline: When Full
# of Vendors: 70
Not a Juried Event
Attendance: 4000
# of Years Held: 26

© *Music 4 Life* - *All Free Downloads*

11/6/2015 - 11/7/2015
Holiday Bazaar at The Naz
1974 E. McAndrews Road, Medford,
OR - Medford, OR
www.mednaz.com
(541) 779-7777

Annual Holiday Bazaar at The Naz held at: Medford First Church of the Nazarene over 90+ Craft & Artisan Booths ALL items handmade, no commercial products.

Breakfast, Lunch, & Dinner Café, Homemade Baked Goods Sale Admission: $1, or 1 non-perishable food item 16 & under FREE portion of our proceeds is given back to our community!

Follow us on facebook:
www.facebook.com/holidaybazaaratthenaz

Paid Admission $1 or 1 non-perishable food item
No Kid's Activities
Hours: Friday, November 6, 10am - 6pm
             Saturday, November 7, 9am - 4pm

Vendor Contact: Jonalyn Fabrin jfabrin@mednaz.com
Deadline: 4/1/15
# of Vendors: 90
Juried Event
Attendance: 3500
# of Years Held: 20

Christmas Decorations
© George Hodan
All Free Downloads

11/6/2015 - 11/7/2015
Snowflake Boutique 2015
Deschutes County Fairgrounds
Redmond, OR
www.snowflakeboutique.org

Part of admission fee benefits Family Access Network (FAN) in Redmand, a network of agencies that provides services to children and families in need.

This is a boutique style bazaar, with one checkout. Everything is juried and handmade. You'll find holiday decor, furniture, clothing, ceramics, soaps, candles, jewelry, one-of-a-kind decorations, quilts and more!

Paid Admission
Hours: Fri: 1pm - 8pm;
       Sat: 9am - 4pm

Vendor Contact:
judiesnowflake@bendbroadband.com
Juried Event
# of Years Held: 40

11/6/2015 - 11/7/2015
St Mary's Arts & Craft Bazaar
706 Ellsworth St SW - Albany, OR
www.stmarysalbany.com/st-marys-arts-crafts-bazaar/

Admission: Not Provided
Hours: Sat: 10-7pm; Sun: 9-5pm

Vendor Contact: stmarys_albany@comcast.net

11/7/2015 - 11/8/2015
70th Annual St. Mary's Arts & Craft Bazaar
St. Mary's Hwy 20 - Albany, OR
(541) 926-6812

Admission: Not Provided
Hours: Fri: 10am - 7pm; Sat: 9am - 5pm

Vendor Contact: Sharon Konopa
stmarysbazaar@comcast.net

11/7/2015 - 11/7/2015
Crafters Market & Home-Based Business Expo
Santiam Place Event Center - Lebanon, OR
www.santiamplace.com   (541) 259-4255

Shop for that special gift. Handmade items make great
gifts and decorations!

Free Admission
Hours: 9am - 4pm

Vendor Contact: Sally Skaggs
blueroofshirts@centurytel.net   Deadline: 10/24/15#
of Vendors: 20   Attendance: 600

11/7/2015 - 11/8/2015
**Crafts on the Coast Harvest & Holiday Arts & Crafts
Festival**
Yachats Commons Building - Yachats, OR
(541) 547-4664

Over 65 vendors with quality handcrafted works and
gourmet food products.

Free Admission   Hours: Sat: 10-5; Sun: 10-4

Vendor Contact: Violet or Jean violet@peak.org
# of Vendors: 65   Juried Event   Attendance: 2000
# of Years Held: 18

11/7/2015 - 11/8/2015
Philomath Holiday Craft Fair
Philomath Elementary - Philomath, OR
www.philomathrodeo.org   (541) 231-9243

Admission: Not Provided
Hours: Sat: 9am-5pm; Sun: 10am-3pm

Vendor Contact: Rusty Root marilyns@peak.org
# of Vendors: 50   # of Years Held: 61

11/7/2015 - 11/18/2015
Philomath Holiday Craft Fair
Philomath Elementary School - 239 S 16th St
Philomath, OR   (541) 740-7955

Admission: Not Provided

Vendor Contact: marilyns@peak.org

11/7/2015 - 11/7/2015
Salem Holiday Craft Bazaar
Bethany Baptist Church - Salem, OR
www.bethanybaptistchurch.com

Free Admission
Hours: 9am - 4pm

Vendor Contact: bethanymopsbazaar@gmail.com
# of Vendors: 50

11/9/2015 - 11/14/2015
Country Christmas 2015
Clackamas County Fairgrounds - Canby, OR
www.countrybazaars.com

Free Admission
Hours: Mon - Fri: am - 8pm; Sat: 9am - 5pm

Vendor Contact: countryjunction@canby.com
# of Vendors: 225   Attendance: 6,000

11/13/2015 - 11/13/2015
Holiday Marketplace 2015
New Hope Community Church - Portland, OR
(503) 659-5683

Admission: Not Provided

11/13/2015 - 11/14/2015
Josephine County Christmas Bazaar
Josephine County Fairgrounds - Grants Pass, OR

First Christmas show of the season for the area.
Admission: Not Provided
Hours: Fri: 9am - 4pm; Sat: 9am - 4pm

# of Vendors: 75   Not a Juried Event
# of Years Held: 2000

11/13/2015 - 11/14/2015
TCF Holiday Bazaar
Tillamook Fairgrounds - Tillamook, OR
www.tillamookfair.com   (503) 842-2472

Admission: Not Provided
Hours: Fri: Noon-7pm; Sat: 10am - 5pm

Vendor Contact: tillamookfair@tillamookfair.com
# of Vendors: 90   Juried Event
Attendance: 2500   # of Years Held: 23

11/14/2015 - 11/14/2015
Beaverton High School Holiday Bazaar
Beaverton High School - 1300 SW 2nd - Beaverton, OR
www.bhsholidaybazaar.myevent.com

Admission: Not Provided
Hours: 10am - 5pm

Vendor Contact: anne_erwin@beaverton.k12.or.us

11/14/2015 - 11/14/2015
Brookings Harbor Community Bazaar
High School and Azalea School, corner of Pacific and
Oak. - Brookings, OR
www.brookingsharborbazaar.com   (541) 469-2093

The Brookings Harbor Community Bazaar began over 45
years ago, providing quality handmade items, and held
in two large venues, back-to-back at the schools. Over
100 vendor booths plus food carts entice the customers
to stay and enjoy. Vendor fees are reasonable and
information is on our web site. This is THE largest, best
bazaar on the southern Oregon Coast. This has become
"Bazaar Saturday," and customers will find other smaller
venues located around town. Local shops join in the fun
too! Vendor registration begins on September 1...see
website for details. Don't miss out on this great event!

Free Admission
Hours: Saturday, November 14, 2015 from 9am to 5pm.

Vendor Contact: Vangie Andreason
info@brookingsharborbazaar.com
Deadline: 9/1/15   # of Vendors: 110
Juried Event
Attendance: 1000   # of Years Held: 45+

11/14/2015 - 12/31/2015
Lighting of Maddax Woods
5785 River St - West Linn, OR   (503) 722-2131

Enjoy the lit paths and wildlife at Maddax Woods park.

Admission: Not Provided
Kid Friendly Event
Hours: Celebration 11/14: 3-8pm; Daily 4-9pm

Vendor Contact: Sally McLarty

11/14/2015 - 11/14/2015
Northwest Food & Wine Festival
Double Tree Hotel at Lloyd Center - Portland, OR
www.nwwinefestival.com
(800) 422-0251, ext. 3006

This legendary wine and food festival represents the Northwest's highest quality wines, spirits, beers and foods.

Admission: Not Provided
Hours: 4pm - 8pm

Vendor Contact: Tina Curry
tina@nwfoodandwinefestival.com

11/14/2015 - 11/15/2015
Old Fashion Christmas in Redmond
Deschutes County Fairgrounds - Sisters, OR
www.centraloregonshows.com   (541) 420-0279

Paid Admission
Kid Friendly Event
Hours: Sat: 10am - 6pm; Sun: 10am - 5pm

Vendor Contact: Richard Esterman
centraloregonshows@gmail.com
# of Years Held: NEW

Snow Bench
© George Hodan
All Free Downloads

11/14/2015 - 11/14/2015
Second Saturday at WAAAM Air
& Auto Museum
1600 Air Museum Road
Hood River, OR

www.waaamuseum.org   541-308-1600

The Second Saturday of each month the WAAAM Air and
Auto Museum opens the doors to roll out and run some
of its antique airplanes and cars. Visitors watch airplane
operations up close and may get to ride in old cars too.
Open 9-5. Activities 10-2. Lunch 11-1. Free parking.
WAAAM is located three miles from downtown Hood
River at 1600 Air Museum Road, Hood River, OR 97031.

Paid Admission
Kid Friendly Event
Hours: Daily 9am-5pm

11/15/2015 - 11/15/2015
Christmas Craft & Small Business Fair
Sutherlin Adventists Christian School - Sutherlin, OR
(541) 617-7018

Admission: Not Provided

Vendor Contact: Terri Wilkinson
teri_a_wilkinson@hotmail.com
# of Vendors: 40

11/15/2015 - 11/16/2015
Southern Oregon Holiday Market
Jackson County Expo - Central Point, OR
www.attheexpo.com   (541) 774-8271

Admission: Not Provided
Hours: Fri: 10am-6pm; Sat: 10am - 5pm

Vendor Contact: Lori Burk

11/16/2015 - 11/21/2015
Every Husband's Nightmare Bazaar
Washington County Fairgrounds - Hillsboro, OR
www.nightmarebazaar.com   (503) 648-1416

This boutique style show features handcrafted wares, antiques, collectibles and groumet foods. The artists come from all over the Northwest. You're sure to find gifts for all the special folks in your life!

Free Admission
Hours: Tues - Fri: 10am - 8pm; Sat: 10am - 5pm

# of Vendors: 200   Attendance: 10000

11/20/2015 - 11/22/2015
Portland Gem Faire
Oregon Convention Center - Portland, OR
www.gemfaire.com   (503) 252-8300

Fine jewelry, precious & semi-precious gemstones, millions of beads, crystals, gold & silver, minerals & much more at manufacturer's prices. Over 70 exhibitors from around the world. Jewelry repair & cleaning while you shop. Free hourly door prizes. For more info, visit www.gemfaire.com or call (503) 252-8300 or email: info@gemfaire.com.

Paid Admission
No Kid's Activities
Hours: Fri Noon-6pm, Sat 10am-6pm, Sun 10am-5pm

Vendor Contact: Allen Van Volkinburgh
info@gemfaire.com
Deadline: Until Full
# of Vendors: 70
Not a Juried Event
Attendance: 4000
# of Years Held: 26

11/21/2015 - 11/21/2015
Holiday Bazaar
Grout Elementary School - 3119 SE Holgate Blvd
Portland, OR   (503) 916-6209

Admission: Not Provided
Vendor Contact: groutbazaar@gmail.com

11/21/2015 - 11/22/2015
Old Fashion Christmas in Salem
Oregon State Fairgrounds - Salem, OR
www.centraloregonshows.com   (541) 420-0279

Paid Admission
Kid Friendly Event
Hours: Sat: 10am - 6pm; Sun: 10am - 5pm

Vendor Contact: Richard Esterman
centraloregonshows@gmail.com

11/21/2015 - 11/21/15 (tentative)
Portland Christian Center's Holiday Gift Market
Portland, OR

Admission: Not Provided

11/21/2015 - 11/22/2015
Santa's Treasures Holiday Bazaar
10955 SE 25th Ave - Milwaukie, OR
www.facebook.com/SantasTreasures
(503) 659-1489

Admission: Not Provided
Hours: Sat: 9am-4pm; Sun: 8am-3pm

Vendor Contact: santastreasures@gmail.com

11/21/2015 - 12/24/2015
Saturday Market's Holiday Market
Lane Events Center, 796 W. 13th - Eugene, OR
www.holidaymarket.org   (541) 686-8885

Eugene's Saturday Market Holiday Market is a weekly celebration of local arts, food and music. 300 artisans sell their handcrafted goods, fifteen food booths serve up an international array of foods, and the stage features six different live music acts each day.

Event is indoors, with a festive holiday atmosphere. Open every Saturday & Sunday from the weekend before Thanksgiving through Christmas eve plus selected weekdays.

Free Admission
Kid Friendly Event
Hours: Weekends only, 10am-6pm

Vendor Contact: Vi Sadhana
visadhana@eugenesaturdaymarket.org
Deadline: 11/10/15
# of Vendors: 250   Juried Event
Attendance: 3,000/day   # of Years Held: 25

11/22/2015 - 11/22/2015
Westminister Holiday Bazaar
Corner of Coburg & Harlow
Westminister Presbyterian Church - Eugene, OR

Free Admission
Hours: 9am - 4pm

Vendor Contact: Nancy Holloman
Deadline: 11/1/15   # of Vendors: 18

11/25/2015 - 12/30/2015
Christmas Festival of the Lights
The Grotto - 8840 NE Skidmore St - Portland, OR
www.thegrotto.org   (503) 254-7371

500,000 lights merrily dance as The Grotto begins its celebration of Christmas.

Event includes 150 choral performances, a petting zoo, carolers, puppet shows, and hot chocolate. This is a very special event for the whole family!

Admission: Not Provided
Kid Friendly Event

11/25/2015 - 1/2/2016
Oregon Zoo ZooLights
4001 SW Canyon Rd - Portland, OR
www.oregonzoo.org   (503) 226-1561

Paid Admission
Kid Friendly Event

Vendor Contact: info@oregonzoo.org

11/26/2015 - 12/31/2015
29th Annual Holiday Lights at Shore Acres
State Park
Shore Acres State Park - Coos Bay, OR
www.shoreacres.net/holiday-lights/

Admission: Not Provided
Kid Friendly Event
Hours: 4pm - 9:30pm

Vendor Contact: bridgham@epuerto.com
Attendance: 45000   # of Years Held: 29

11/26/2015 - 11/30/2015
Cascade Health Festival of Trees
Valley River Inn - Eugene, OR
http://www.cascadehealth.org/festival-of-trees/
(541) 228-3040

Admission: Not Provided
Kid Friendly Event
Hours: See schedule on website

11/26/2015 - 11/26/2015
Macy's Parde / Holiday Christmas Tree Lighting
Downtown - Portland, OR

Free Admission
Kid Friendly Event

11/27/2015 - 12/6/2015
America's Greatest Christmas Bazaar
Portland Expo Center - Portland, OR
www.expochristmasbazaar.com

Paid Admission
Hours: Two Big Weekends
        Fridays & Saturdays: 10am-6pm;
        Sundays: 10am - 5pm

Vendor Contact: elves@expochristmasbazaar.com
# of Vendors: 600+   Attendance: 33,000
# of Years Held: 33

---

*Our hearts grow tender with childhood memories of love of
kindred, and we are better throughout the year for having, in
spirit, become a child again at Christmas-time.*
~~Laura Ingals Wilder 1867 - 1957

11/27/2015 - 1/3/2016
Christmas in the Garden
The Oregon Garden - Silverton, OR
www.oregongarden.org/events/christmas-in-the-garden/   503-874-8100

Enjoy Christmas lights, artisan vendors, fire pits, carolers, photos with Santa and festive food, all set in the charming Rediscovery Forest, Thursdays - Sundays, Nov. 27 - Dec. 20.

Paid Admission
Kid Friendly Event
Hours: 4pm - 9pm

Vendor Contact: Mary Ridderbusch-Shearer
info@oregongarden.org
Deadline: September
# of Vendors: varies   Not a Juried Event
Attendance: 22500   # of Years Held: 3

11/27/2015 - 11/27/2015
Festival of Lights
Downtown - Ashland, OR

Free Admission
Kid Friendly Event

11/27/2015 - 11/28/2015
Rickreall Craft Festival
Polk County Fairgrounds - Rickreall, OR
www.co.polk.or.us   (503) 623-3048

Two buildings full of handmade items from local artisans.

Free Admission
Hours: 9am - 5pm

Vendor Contact: Linda Friedow
friedow.linda@co.polk.or.us
# of Vendors: 150   Attendance: 3000

11/27/2015 - 11/29/2015
Seaside Holiday Gift Fair & Parade
Seaside Civic & Convention Center - Seaside, OR
www.seasidechamber.com/events/events-
2/holiday-gift-fair/   (503) 440-7168

Admission: Not Provided
Kid Friendly Event
Hours: Fri: noon - 5pm;
        Sat: 10am - 4pm;
        Sun: 10a - 3pm

Vendor Contact: Cyndi Mudge cyndi@mudge3m.com
Deadline: 9/7/15   # of Vendors: 70
# of Years Held: 30

11/27/2015 - 11/27/2015
Starlight Parade
404 W 2nd St - The Dalles, OR
(541) 296-2231

This lighted parade kicks off the holiday season! Take a
picture with Santa inside the Chamber of Commerce
building, and don't forget there's hot chocolate or coffee!

Free Admission
Kid Friendly Event
Hours: 6pm

11/27/2015 - 11/27/2015
Tree Lighting Ceremony Presented by SmartPark
Pioneer Courthouse Square - Downtown - Portland, OR

Ring in the holidays with the annual tree lighting.

Free Admission
Kid Friendly Event

11/28/2015 - 11/29/2015
11th Hour Santa Craft Sale
540 NE Hwy 101 - Lincoln City, OR
(541) 994-9994

You'll save money on unique gifts for friends and family this Christmas at the "11th Hour Santa" show! Proceeds benefit the Cultural Center.

Admission: Not Provided
Hours: Fri: Noon - 7pm; Sat: 10am-4pm

11/28/2015 - 12/13/2015
Home for the Holidays
Centennial Park - SW 7th St - Redmond, OR

Admission: Not Provided
Hours: Every Fri & Saturday; 11am - 5pm

...It came without ribbons! It came without tags! It came without packages, boxes or bags!... Then the Grinch thought of somethine he hadn't before! Maybe Christmas, he thought, doesn't come from a store. Maybe Christmas... perhaps... means a little bit more!
~~ Dr. Seuss (1904-1991), How the Grinch Stole Christmas!

Winter Landscapes © Larisa Koshkina
All Free Downloads

December 2015

12/2/2015 - 12/27/2015
A Christmas Carol
Portland Playhouse - Portland, OR
www.portlandplayhouse.org

The beloved tale by Charles Dickens comes to life in Portland each year! It is a not to be missed annual Christmas tradition.

Admission: Not Provided
Kid Friendly Event

12/2/2015 - 12/30/2015
Christmas Fantasy Trail Wenzel Farm
19754 So. Ridge Road - Oregon City, OR
www.fantasytrail.com   (503) 631-2047

Take a walk through a lighted, wooded "FANTASY TRAIL' decorated with spooky sights and sounds at Halloween, decorated with thousands of lights for your Christmas enchantment. Also, walk through 40' castle with Halloween and Christmas scenes. Have fun on suspension bridge, walk through tunnel, maze or crooked house! Bonfire nightly at Christmas. Everything is geared in age from 0 - 100 years. Great for families.

Halloween Fantasy Trail will be celebrating its 21st year while Christmas Fantasy Trail will be celebrating its 23rd year.

Paid Admission
Kid Friendly Event
Hours: See website for days and hours of operation
# of Years Held: 23 years

12/2/2015 - 12/6/2015
Holiday Ale Festival
Pioneer Courthouse Square - Downtown - Portland, OR
www.holidayale.com

Paid Admission
No Kid's Activities
Hours: Wed - Sat: 11am-10pm; Sun: 11am-5pm

12/4/2015 - 12/5/2015
Christmas in Dairyville
Alpenrose Dairy - Portland, OR
www.alpenrose.com   (503) 452-2139

This Ho Ho Ho Holiday tradition is a must see at
Dairyville, a replica of a western frontier town. This fun
place is transformed into a winter wonderland, with
animal displays, vintage storefronts, local choirs, holiday
movies and, of course, Santa Claus!

Admission: Not Provided   Kid Friendly Event

Vendor Contact: Tracey McKinnon
tracey@alpenrose.com

12/4/2015 - 12/20/2015
Christmas Ship Parade - Columbia River
Columbia River - Portland, OR
www.christmasships.org

Free Admission   Kid Friendly Event
Hours: See Online Schedule

12/4/2015 - 12/20/2015
Christmas Ship Parade - Willamette River
Willamette River - Portland, OR
www.christmasships.org

Free Admission
Kid Friendly Event   Hours: See Online Schedule

Christmas
StoryBook
Land

12/4/2015 - 12/18/2015
Christmas
Land
Linn County Fair & Expo Center - Cascade
Livestock Building - Albany, OR
www.christmasstorybookland.org
(541) 928-4546

Take a stimulated walk through the woods to see over 90 scaled down scenes of Mother Goose rhyme characters, children's fairy tale characters, family movie scenes plus two model trains and Victorian Village. Then visit Santa for a free candy cane!

A Portland tradition every Christmas!

Free Admission
Kid Friendly Event
Hours: Mon-Fri 6:30pm-8:30pm;
        Sat & Sun: 10am-8:30pm;
        Dec 11th Special hours: 3pm-8:30pm;
        Dec 18th Special hours: 1pm-8:30pm

Vendor Contact: Carol Wood
ChristmasStorybookLand@gmail.com
# of Years Held: 39

It's Christmas eve and snowflakes are falling upon a green tree that is twinkling with lights, all around the carols are calling their songs wrapped in love warm the night!

The wonder of children, the sweet simple pleasures, the joy that surrounds you where ever you go! This is the season that brings us such treasures… open your heart and let the love in!
~~ Catherine Pittman © 1995 "Christmas Eve" from the album, The Magic of Christmas

12/4/2015 - 12/6/2015
Douglas County Christmas Craft Fair
Douglas County Fairgrounds - Roseburg, OR
www.co.douglas.or.us   (541) 440-4394

The largest and most popular Christmas fair in southern Oregon. 300+ exhibitors display a wide variety of handmade items, such as clothing, décor, baked goods, spices, gourmet coffees, wood crafts, metal sculptures, and many, many more unique products!

Admission: Not Provided
Hours: Fri & Sat: 10am - 8pm;
         Sun: 10am - 5pm

Vendor Contact: Ciera Keith
# of Vendors: 300   Juried Event
Attendance: 11000   # of Years Held: 43

12/4/2015 - 12/6/2015
Follow the Star Living Nativity
Gladstone Park Conference Center - Gladstone, OR
www.gladstonepark.org/followthestar

Free Admission
Kid Friendly Event
Hours: Friday Gates Open: 5:30 pm;
         Saturday & Sunday: 4:30 pm

12/4/2015 - 12/5/2015
Funky Junk Sisters: Rebel Junk
Washington County Fairgrounds - Hillsboro, OR
www.funkyjunksisters.com

Admission: Not Provided

Vendor Contact: funkyjunksisters@live.com

12/4/2015 - 12/4/2015
Hood River Holidays
Downtown - Hood River, OR
www.hoodriver.org   (541) 386-2000

Free Admission
Kid Friendly Event
Hours: 5pm - 7pm

Vendor Contact: info@hoodriver.org

12/4/2015 - 12/5/2015
Leach Botanical Garden Holiday Bazaar &
Artist Market
Leach Botanical Garden, 6704 SE 122nd Ave.
Portland, OR
www.leachgarden.org   (503) 823-1671

A great way to support the Garden and kick off your
holiday season. Our festive holiday event features
freshly made wreaths, swags, centerpieces, cut greens,
baked goods & an Artist Market featuring work by local
glass, ceramic, metal, and fabric artists!

Come experience the winter garden, sip hot cider in the
historic Manor House, and enjoy holiday music while you
shop.

Free Admission
Hours: 9am - 3pm
Not a Juried Event

Once upon a time, a star rose high in the sky...
It shined both morning and night.
And the little star made the darkness take its flight,
Over Bethlehem, it took rest.
"Tell me what it means," I asked the shepherd boy,
He answered very softly, "it's God's promise of hope."
~~ Catherine Pittman © 1995 First Christmas from the album
The Magic of Christmas

12/4/2015 - 12/5/2015
OSU Holiday Marketplace
OSU Craft Center - 2251 SW
Jefferson St - Corvallis, OR

www.mu.oregonstate.edu/craft-center/holiday-marketplace
(541) 737-2937

Free Admission
Hours: 10am - 6pm

# of Vendors: 60   Juried Event
Attendance: 6000

12/4/2015 - 12/5/2015
Providence Festival of Trees - Portland
Oregon Convention Center - Portland, OR
www.oregon.providence.org/our-services/p/providence-festival-of-trees-portland/
(503) 216-6625

Paid Admission
Kid Friendly Event
Hours: Fri: 10:30am - 5pm; Sat: 9am-5pm

12/5/2015 - 12/5/2015
A Whale of Christmas in Depoe Bay
Whale Watching Center - 119 SW Hwy 101
Depoe Bay, OR   (541) 765-2889

Ring in the holidays with the annual Christmas tree lighting! Then visit the downtown area as it comes alive with holiday splendor. Vendors, kids entertainment, food and live music!

Free Admission
Kid Friendly Event

12/5/2015 - 12/5/2015
Bend Christmas Parade
Downtown Bend - Bend, OR
www.3gcreativestudio.com/bcp/   (541) 383-3879

Admission: Not Provided
Kid Friendly Event

Vendor Contact: Dina Barker Ernie Gilpin
# of Years Held: 24

12/5/2015 - 12/5/2015
Ceramic Ornament Painting
Spark Arts Center, 1805 NE Cesar Chavez Bld, Portland,
OR, 97212 - Portland, OR
www.sparkartscenter.com   (503) 281-6757

Create and paint your own design on a ceramic
ornament to give or keep for yourself!

Paid Admission
Kid Friendly Event
Hours: Saturday, 10am - 2pm

12/5/2015 - 12/5/15 (tentative)
David Douglas HS 18th Holiday Bazaar 2015
1001 SE 135th St - Portland, OR
www.daviddouglashighschool.my-pta.org

Proceeds support the DDHS PTSA College Scholarship
Fund.

Admission: Not Provided
Kid Friendly Event
Hours: 9am - 4pm

# of Vendors: 100   Attendance: 500
# of Years Held: 19

12/5/2015 - 12/5/15 (Tentative)
Garden Home Recreation Center Holiday Bazaar
7475 SW Oleson Rd - Portland, OR
(503) 629-6341

Admission: Not Provided
Hours: 9am - 4pm

# of Years Held: 31

12/5/2015 - 12/5/2015
Hawthorne Holiday Stroll
SE Hawthorne - Portland, OR
www.hathornepdx.com

Free Admission
Hours: 11am - 6pm

Vendor Contact: explore@thinkhawthorne.com

12/5/2015 - 12/5/2015
Keerin's Hall Holiday Bazaar
Grant County Fairgrounds - John Day, OR
www.grantcountyfairgrounds.com/events.php/12
(541) 575-1900

Held in conjunction with the Blue Mountain Hospital
Auxilary Bazaar

Free Admission

It's time to deck the halls with holly, hang the mistletoe,
It's time to send those Christmas greetings,
Here is how one goes...
We wish you a Merry Christmas,
We wish you a Merry Christmas,
We wish you a Merry Christmas and a Happy New Year!
Let's trim the trim with twinkling lights,
Hang your stockings Christmas night,
Share the magic of the Christmas season... Come one and all!
~~ Catherine Pittman © 1995 additional lyrics to We Wish You
a Merry Christmas from the album The Magic of Christmas

12/5/2015 - 12/6/2015
Klamath Falls Christmas Bazaar & Craft Fair
Klamath County Fairgrounds - Klamath Falls, OR
(541) 883-3796

Admission: Not Provided
Hours: Sat: 9am - tpm; Sun: 10am - 4pm

Vendor Contact: Fran Coker
auntfranniesattic@gmail.com
# of Vendors: 100   Juried Event
Attendance: 4000   # of Years Held: 47

12/5/2015 - 12/5/15
Lewis Elementary Holiday Bazaar 2015
4401 SE Evergreen School Gym – Portland, OR

Admission: Not Provided

Silver bells and twinkling lights,
Stars that brighten winter nights,
The magic of Christmas has come!
Snowflakes tickle reindeer feet,
Carols ring on every street,
These magic joys Christmas brings!
Children with their cheeks aglow,
Snowmen tip a hat hello,
Christmas is here little ones!
Stockings hung with loving hands,
Outside a winter wonderland,
Come celebrate it with me!
Love and laughter fill the air,
Christmas dreams come true,
Angels bless the sleeping lamb,
May good blessings find you too!

~~ Catherine Pittman © 1995 Title Song Lyrics from the album
The Magic of Christmas

12/5/2015 - 12/6/2015
Quota Christmas Bazaar and Craft Fair
Klamath County Fairgrounds, Buildings #1 and #2 -
Klamath Falls, OR   (541) 281-5994

Quota International of Klamath Falls presents the 48th annual Christmas Bazaar and Craft Fair. Nearly 100 booths offer a wide selection of handcrafted items and other gift products. Free admission, donations appreciated. Photos with Santa, Treasure Hunt Raffle, Concessions also provided.

We collect new pajamas for children in foster care. This event provides funding for organizations assisting disadvantaged women and children, as well as helping the deaf and hard of hearing.

Free Admission
Kid Friendly Event
Hours: Sat. December 5th - 9am - 5pm Sun. December 6th - 10am 4pm

Vendor Contact: Fran Coker francoker.1@gmail.com
Deadline: 9/30/15
# of Vendors: 99   Not a Juried Event
Attendance: 2000   # of Years Held: 48

12/5/2015 - 12/6/2015
ScanFair 2015
Portland Veterans Memorial Coliseum - Portland, OR
www.scanheritage.org   (503) 977-0275

Paid Admission
Hours: Sat: 10am-5pm; Sun: 10am-4pm

Vendor Contact: shf@mindspring.com

12/5/2015 - 12/5/2015
Wilkes Holiday Bazaar
Wilkes Elementary - 17020 NE Wilkes Rd - Portland, OR
www.reynolds.k12.or.us/wilkes/wilkes-holiday-
bazaar   (503) 255-6133

Admission: Not Provided
Vendor Contact: robin_wooley@reynolds.k12.or.us

12/6/2015 - 12/8/2015
Christmas Showcase
Jackson County Expo - Central Point, OR
www.attheexpo.com   (541) 774-8271

Admission: Not Provided
Hours: Fri & Sat: 10am-5pm; Sun: 10am-4pm

Vendor Contact: Lori Burk

12/6/2015 - 12/6/2015
Laurelhurst Winter Bazaar
Laurelhurst School - 840 NE 4126 Ave - Portland, OR
www.facebook.com/laurelhurstbazaar

Admission: Not Provided
Hours: 9am - 4pm

12/6/2015 - 12/8/2015
Town & Country Christmas Bazaar
Linn County Fairgrounds - Albany, OR
www.lcfairexpo.com/christmas.bazaar.html
(541) 926-4314

Paid Admission
Hours: Fri: Noon - 8pm;
        Sat: 10am - 6p;
        Sun: 10am - 4pm

Vendor Contact: Cathy Exline
# of Vendors: 200

12/8/2015 - 12/10/2015
Portland Artisan Market - Holiday Market
Pioneer Courthouse Square - Downtown - Portland, OR

This annual holiday market features 40 artisans selling their wares! You'll find plenty of great handmade items for your holiday décor and gift-giving!

Free Admission
# of Vendors: 40

12/11/2015 - 12/13/2015
Follow the Star Living Nativity
Gladstone Park Conference Center - Gladstone, OR
www.gladstonepark.org/followthestar

Free Admission
Kid Friendly Event
Hours: Friday Gates Open: 5:30 pm;
           Saturday & Sunday: 4:30 pm

12/11/2015 - 12/13/2015
Green Festival
Oregon Convention Center - Portland, OR
www.greenfestivals.com   (828) 236-0324

Paid Admission

12/12/2015 - 12/13/2015
Last Chance Holiday Bazaar
Hood River County Fairgrounds - Hood River, OR
www.hoodriverfair.org   (541) 354-2865

Admission: Not Provided
Hours: 10a - 4pm

Vendor Contact: hrfair@hrecn.net

12/12/2015 - 12/12/2015
Riddle Christmas Craft Fair
Riddle Community Center - Riddle, OR
(541) 476-4021

Free Admission
Vendor Contact: Alysen Sylvester
amento975@msn.com
# of Vendors: 29

12/12/2015 - 12/13/2015
Salem Holiday Gift Market
Oregon State Fairgrounds - Salem, OR
www.salemsaturdaymarket.com   (503) 585-8264

Admission: Not Provided
Hours: Sat: 10am-6pm; Sun: 10am-4pm

Vendor Contact: info@salemsaturdaymarket.com
Deadline: 9/1/15
# of Vendors: 200   Juried Event
Attendance: 15000

12/12/2015 - 12/12/2015
Second Saturday at WAAAM Air & Auto Museum
1600 Air Museum Road
Hood River, OR

www.waaamuseum.org   541-308-1600

The Second Saturday of each month the WAAAM Air and Auto Museum opens the doors to roll out and run some of its antique airplanes and cars. Visitors watch airplane operations up close and may get to ride in old cars too. Open 9-5. Activities 10-2. Lunch 11-1. Free parking. WAAAM is located three miles from downtown Hood River at 1600 Air Museum Road, Hood River, OR 97031.

Paid Admission
Kid Friendly Event   Hours: Daily 9am-5pm

12/12/2015 - 12/13/2015
Super Colossal Holiday Sale
Oregon Convention Center - Exhibit Hall D - Portland, OR
(503) 224-9097

Free Admission
Kid Friendly Event
Hours: 11am - 6pm

Vendor Contact: craftywonderland@yahoo.com
# of Vendors: 200

12/13/2015 - 12/13/2015
Christmas Trains
McEwen Depot - Baker City, OR
www.sumptervalleyrailroad.org

Take a trip back in time through a winter wonderland
while enjoying a steam-powered train. Visit with Santa,
warm-up with free cocoa, coffe or cider, go shopping at
the Sumpter Christmas Bazaar!   Fun for the whole
family.

Paid Admission
Kid Friendly Event
Hours: Departs from McEwen 10am and 1:15 pm,
         Round trip from Sumpter at noon.
         Evening lights train departing at 4:15 pm
         for the Sumpter tree lighting & parade.

Vendor Contact: info@sumptervalleyrailroad.org

---

*Christmas waves a magic wang over this world, and behold,
everything is softer and more beautiful.*
~~ Norman Vincent Peale, Minister & Author 1898 – 1993

12/14/2015 - 12/31/2015
Peacock Lane Christmas Lights
Peacock Lane: Between Stark St and SE Belmont St and one block east of SE 39th. - Portland, OR
www.peacocklane.net

 have decorated each house. Most of the homes in this quaint southeast neighborhood are Tudor homes. Street has beautiful sparkling lights, nativity scenes, Christmas trees, life-like replicas of Santa and Frosty. Warning: This is a very popular tradition. It is wise to park several blocks away and walk the display rather than driving through the area.

Free Admission
Kid Friendly Event
Hours: 6pm - 11pm

Vendor Contact: peacocklane@comcast.net
# of Years Held: 95

Oh shepherd boy,
where are you going with
your flock of sheep?
I follow the bright star
above to see just where it
leads.

Oh mighty king,
With all your treasures,
why follow the bright star?

In a place called Bethlehem, there is a child of God.

A baby born, to bring us peace on this Christmas day,
Heaven blessed the sleeping child,
While in a manger bed he lay...
~~Catherine Pittman © 1995
from the album The Magic of Christmas

Photo by Public Domain Pictures
All Free Downloads

January 2016

1/22/2016 - 1/24/2016
11th Good Earth Home, Garden & Living Show
Lane Co Convention Center - Fairgrounds - Eugene, OR
www.EugeneHomeshow.com   (541) 484-9247

America's 1st Sustainable Home & Garden Show
Returns! Over 250 Sustainable Exhibits for the Home,
Garden & Life. Explore 7 Pavilions of Green Good Earth
Living: Home, Garden, Food, Transportation, Art,
Wellness, and ReUse. Enjoy National Green Building
Experts, Sustainable Living Experts, NW Authors, Live
Music, Organic Eats, 80 Eco-Friendly Seminars, Green
Neighbors, and Our Signature Chickens Over the Aisles!
FREE parking.

Free Admission with canned food donations
Kid Friendly Event
Hours: Fri: 5pm-9pm, Sat: 10am-8pm, Sun: 10am-5pm

Vendor Contact: Beth Little
info@eugenehomeshow.com
Deadline: When Full   # of Vendors: 342
Juried Event   # of Years Held: 10

1/22/2016 - 1/24/2016
Good Earth Home, Garden & Living Show
Lane Events Center - Eugene, OR
www.eugenehomeshow.com   (541) 484-9247

Paid Admission
Vendor Contact: info@eugenehomeshow.com

1/9/2016 - 1/10/2016
Curious Gallery 2016
Crowne Plaza - Portland, OR
www.curiousgallerypdx.com

Paid Admission
Vendor Contact: curiousgallerypdx@gmail.com

1/9/2016 - 1/9/2016
Second Saturday at WAAAM Air & Auto Museum
1600 Air Museum Road
Hood River, OR

www.waaamuseum.org   541-308-1600

The Second Saturday of each month the WAAAM Air and Auto Museum opens the doors to roll out and run some of its antique airplanes and cars. Visitors watch airplane operations up close and may get to ride in old cars too. Open 9-5. Activities 10-2. Lunch 11-1.

Free parking. WAAAM is located three miles from downtown Hood River at 1600 Air Museum Road, Hood River, OR 97031.

Paid Admission
Kid Friendly Event
Hours: Daily 9am-5pm

1/13/2016 - 1/17/2016
Portland Boat Show
Portland Expo Center - Portland, OR
www.otshows.com   (800) 343-6973

Paid Admission
Vendor Contact: info@otshows.com

1/16/2016 - 1/17/2016
5th Annual Yachats Agate Festival
Yachats Visitor Center - Yachats, OR
(800) 929-0477

Admission: Not Provided
Hours: 10am - 4pm

1/16/2016 - 1/31/2016
Oregon Truffle Festival
Willamette Valley - multiple, OR
www.oregontrufflefestival.com   (888) 695-6659

The first event of its kind in North America, OTF features weekend and a la carte events designed to showcase Oregon's rich and diverse winter bounty with native black and white truffles in the hands of renowned chefs. Enjoy spectacular food and wine pairings, truffle hunts with truffle dogs, truffle dog training, Truffle Growers' Forum, and fresh truffle marketplaces in locations throughout Oregon's Willamette Valley. 2016 festivities will begin with the 2nd annual North American Truffle Dog Championship, the Joriad.

Paid Admission
# of Years Held: 11

*...We ought to walk through the rooms of our lives... not looking
for flaws, but for potential.*
~~Ellen Goodman, American Journalist

*For last year's words belong to last year's language,
And next year's words await another voice.
And to make an end is to make a beginning.*
~~ T.S. Eliot from Little Gidding 1888-1965

1/22/2016 - 1/24/2016
Stitches in Bloom Quilt Show
The Oregon Garden - Silverton, OR
www.oregongarden.org/events/quiltshow/
503-874-8100

Mark your calendar for the 2016 Stitches in Bloom Quilt Show presented by Hope Village, January 22-24, 2016! The show will feature more than 150 beautiful quilts, vendors selling quilting wares, lectures by featured artists and demonstrations by quilting vendors.

Paid Admission
Kid Friendly Event
Hours: 10am - 4pm

Vendor Contact: Mary Ridderbusch-Shearer
info@oregongarden.org
Deadline: April
# of Vendors: varies   Not a Juried Event
Attendance: 2000   # of Years Held: 8

1/23/2016 - 1/24/2016
Oregon Wedding Showcase
Lane Events Center - Eugene, OR
www.oregonweddingshowcase.com
(503) 838-2226

Paid Admission
Vendor Contact:
info@oregonweddingshowcase.com

It is the life of the crystal, the architect of the flake, the fire of the frost, the soul of the sunbeam. This crisp winter air is full of it. ~~ John Burroughs, American essayist 1837 – 1921 from "Winter Sunshine"

1/30/2016 - 1/30/2016
Yachats Lions Annual Crab Feed
Yachats Commons - Yachats, OR   (541) 563-5629

All you can eat crab at this annual family-friendly tradition, along with garlic break, cole slaw, baked beans, coffee or soda.

Paid Admission
Kid Friendly Event
Hours: Begins 12:30 pm

Vendor Contact: Kevin or Peggy
lionscrabfeed2015@gmail.com

01/2016 - TBA
Florence Winter Folk Festival
Florence Events Center - Florence, OR
www.winterfolkfestival.org   (888) 968-4086

Paid Admission
Vendor Contact: winterfolkfest@gmail.com

The clock has struck midnight...
Another new year approaches so swiftly a new day draws near!
May this new year bring many joys to you,
And the Lord bless and keep you all year through.

It's one after midnight... a new year's begun!
With hope its wing and joy 'neath its sun.
What will we see in this baby new year,
I pray love and laughter will be near.
~~ Catherine Pittman © 1995 from the album
The Magic of Christmas

February 2016

2/5/2016 - 2/6/2016
11th Annual Seafood & Wine Festival
Oregon Convention Center - Portland, OR
www.pdxseafoodandwinefestival.com

Paid Admission

2/5/2016 - 2/6/2016
Funky Junk Sisters: Rebel Junk
Washington County Fairgrounds - Hillsboro, OR
www.funkyjunksisters.com

Admission: Not Provided
Vendor Contact: funkyjunksisters@live.com

2/6/2016 - 2/6/2016
Riona's Cave of Treasures
Double Tree Exhibitors Hall: 1000 NE Multnomah St
Portland, OR
www.rionascaveoftreasures.com

Admission: Not Provided
Vendor Contact: ceolannchicabee@yahoo.com

Kisses are a better fate than wisdom.
~~ E.E. Cummings, Poet 1894 – 1962

Grow old with me!
The best is yet to be.
~~ Robert Browning, Poet 1812 – 1889

Love looks not with the eyes, but with the mind,
And therefore is winged Cupid painted blind.
~~ William Shakespeare, Mid-Summer Night's Dream, 1595

Love is like a dew that falls on both nettles and lilies.
~~ Swedish Proverb

2/13/2016 - 2/13/2016
Second Saturday at WAAAM
Air & Auto Museum
1600 Air Museum Road
Hood River, OR

www.waaamuseum.org   541-308-1600

The Second Saturday of each month the WAAAM Air and Auto Museum opens the doors to roll out and run some of its antique airplanes and cars. Visitors watch airplane operations up close and may get to ride in old cars too. Open 9-5. Activities 10-2. Lunch 11-1. Free parking. WAAAM is located three miles from downtown Hood River at 1600 Air Museum Road, Hood River, OR 97031.

Paid Admission
Kid Friendly Event
Hours: Daily 9am-5pm

2/14/2016 - 2/14/2016
St. Valentine's Wedding Voe Renewal Ceremony
Little Log Church - Yachats, OR
(541) 547-4547 or (541) 547-3976

A wonderful ceremony for couples to renew their vows in a group setting. There are two ceremonies. Contact us for times.

Admission: Not Provided
Hours: TBA

2/20/2016 - 2/21/2016
KidFest
Portland Expo Center - Portland, OR
www.kidfestnw.com   (360) 514-0767

Paid Admission
Kid Friendly Event
Hours: 11 - 4; VIP Entry 10am
Vendor Contact: Lori lori@pintsizedproductions.com

3/2016 - 3/2016 - TBD
Brookwood Elementary 2016 Spring Bazaar
3960 SE Cedar St - Hillsboro, OR
www.schools.hsd.k12.or.us/brookwood/BoosterCl
ub/BazaarandBookFair/tabid/4228/Default.aspx
(503) 640-1039

Admission: Not Provided
Vendor Contact: searamics@aol.com

3/1/2016 - 12/24/2016
Portland Saturday Market 2016
Downtown Portland - Portland, OR
www.portlandsaturdaymarket.com (503) 222-6072

Portland's beloved market is celebrating its 42nd season
this year! This ithe Rose City's largest outdoor arts and
craft market for Northwet artisans to show off their skills
and sell their handmade items.

Market includes live music, exotic foods, and plenty of
handmade arts and crafts!

Free Admission
Hours: Sat: 10am - 5pm;
        Sun: 11am - 4:30pm

Vendor Contact: reid@saturdaymarket.org
# of Vendors: 350
# of Years Held: 42

3/10/2016 - 3/13/2016
37th Lane County Home & Garden Show
Lane Co Convention Center - Fairgrounds - Eugene, OR
www.EugeneHomeshow.com   (541) 484-9247

Springtime on every Aisle! Shop & compare 325 exhibits featuring experts, products and services for homes & yards.

Learn How-to's at 50 home & garden seminars. Enjoy Showcase Gardens in Full Bloom, Big Plant Sales, Prize Drawings, and Remodel-it Now.

FREE admission with canned food donations.   FREE Parking. Thurs: 5pm-9pm, Fri: 5pm-9pm, Sat: 10am-8pm, Sun: 10am-5pm www.EugeneHomeShow.com

Free Admission with Canned Food Donations
No Kid's Activities
Hours: Thurs: 5pm-9pm,
        Fri: 5pm-9pm,
        Sat: 10am-8pm,
        Sun: 10am-5pm
        Office is open M-F 9-5

Vendor Contact: Beth Little
info@eugenehomeshow.com
Deadline: When Full
# of Vendors: 480   Juried Event

Attendance: 30,000
# of Years Held: 36

3/12/2016 - 3/12/2016
Second Saturday at WAAAM Air
& Auto Museum
1600 Air Museum Road
Hood River, OR

www.waaamuseum.org   541-308-1600

The Second Saturday of each month the WAAAM Air and Auto Museum opens the doors to roll out and run some of its antique airplanes and cars. Visitors watch airplane operations up close and may get to ride in old cars too. Open 9-5. Activities 10-2. Lunch 11-1. Free parking. WAAAM is located three miles from downtown Hood River at 1600 Air Museum Road, Hood River, OR 97031.

Paid Admission
Kid Friendly Event
Hours: Daily 9am-5pm

3/17/2016 - 3/17/2016
St. Patrick's Day 2016
Various Pubs - Portland, OR
www.oregonirishclub.org   (503) 286-4812

Admission: Not Provided   No Kid's Activities

3/19/2016 - 3/20/2016
14th Annual Spring Craft Bazaar &
Saturday Luncheon
YLC Clubhouse - W 3rd and Pontiac - Yachats, OR
(541) 547-3205

Features a luncheon with pie and beverage options. Fair includes handcrafted items.

Admission: Not Provided
Hours: 10 am - 3pm. Sat Luncheon: 11am - 2pm

Vendor Contact: Sandy Duncan
# of Years Held: 14

3/19/2016 - 3/20/2016
46th Annual Original Yachats Arts & Crafts Fair
Yachats Commons - Yachats, OR
(541) 547-3530 or (800) 929-0477

This annual fair hand-picks 65 of the Pacific Northwest's artisans for their art. Media includes paintings, jewelry, art glass, pottery, furniture, water features, woodwork, clay, sculptures, stained glass, fiber textiles, screen prints, garden art, toys, and more!

Admission: Not Provided
Hours: Sat: 10am - 5pm; Sun: 10am - 4pm

Vendor Contact: info@yachats.org
# of Vendors: 65   Juried Event
# of Years Held: 46

3/20/2016 - 3/26/2016
Spring Whale Watching Week
Cape Perpetua Vistor's Center & Cook's Chasm
Yachats, OR   (541) 765-3304

Admission: Not Provided
Kid Friendly Event
Hours: 10am - 1pm

Vendor Contact: Morris Grover

3/25/2016 - 5/2/2016
Wooden Shoe Tulip Festival
Wooden Shoe Tulip Farm - Woodburn, OR
www.woodenshoe.com   (800) 711-2006

Admission: Not Provided
Kid Friendly Event

Vendor Contact: office@woodenshoe.com

3/26/2016 - 3/27/2016
14th Annual Spring Craft Bazaar &
Saturday Luncheon
YLC Clubhouse - W 3rd and Pontiac - Yachats, OR
(541) 547-3205

Presented by the Yachats Ladies Club members. Features a luncheon with pie and beverage options. Fair includes handcrafted items.

Admission: Not Provided
Hours: 10 am - 3pm. Sat Luncheon: 11am - 2pm

Vendor Contact: Sandy Duncan
# of Years Held: 14

3/26/2016 - 3/26/2016
Annual Easter Egg Hunt
Yachats Community Presbyterian Church - 360 W 7th St
Yachats, OR

Admission: Not Provided
Kid Friendly Event
Hours: 10am

3/27/2016 - 3/27/2016
Alpenrose Easter Egg Hunt
Alpenrose Dairy - Portland, OR
www.alpenrose.com   (503) 452-2139

What child doesn't love a good ol' fashion Easter egg hunt? Tons of prices, including 6-foot bunnies. This is one of the biggest and most anticipated Easter egg hunt west of the Mississippi!

Admission: Not Provided
Kid Friendly Event

Vendor Contact: Tracey McKinnon
tracey@alpenrose.com

4/2/2016 - 4/2/2016
Spring Plant Sale
Leach Botanical Garden, 6704 SE 122nd Ave. Portland
OR 97236 - Portland, OR
www.leachgarden.org   (503) 823-1671

Join us for an exciting selection of unique plants from specialty nurseries and the Garden's own collection. In addition to a wide range of trees, shrubs, perennials, and northwest natives, plant enthusiasts will find diminutive bonsai, lovely carnivorous plants, and an amazing variety of hardy succulents. Hundreds of individual plants from species in the Leach collection have been propagated for this sale.

Participating vendors varies per year but has included: Arbutus Garden Arts, Gresham Japanese Garden, Humble Roots Farm and Nursery, Sedum Chicks, Tide Creek Nursery, Wild Ginger Farm.

Free Admission
Hours: first Saturday April 2016, from 9:30am - 2:00pm

4/4/2016 - 4/9/2016
Spring in the Country Bazaar
Clackamas County Fairgrounds - Canby, OR
www.countrybazaars.com

Free Admission
Hours: Mon - Fri: am - 8pm; Sat: 9am - 5pm

Vendor Contact: countryjunction@canby.com
# of Vendors: 100

4/8/2016 - 04/09/16 (Tentative)
Pear Blossom Street Fair
Downtown Medford - Medford, OR
www.pearblossomparade.org   (541) 890-1828

Admission: Not Provided
Kid Friendly Event

Vendor Contact:
pearblossom@pearblossomparade.org

4/9/2016 - 4/24/16 (tentative)
Blossom Time
Various Hood River County Locations - Hood River, OR
www.hoodriver.org

Come enjoy the blossoming cherry and apple orchards in Hood River County.

This 3-week event offers a gorgeous 35-mile drive along the county's Scenic Tour Route, with thousands of pink and white fruit tree blossoms along the way.

Activities include craft and quilt shows, pancake breakfasts, pansy party, grange blossom dinner, wine and beer tasting, baked goods, preserves and plenty of fresh produce!

Admission: Not Provided

The year's at the spring,
And day's at the morn;
Morning's at seven;
The hillside's dew-pearled;
The lark's on the wing;
The snail's on the thorn;
God's in His heaven-
All's right with the world!
~~ Robert Browning, Poet 1812 - 1869

4/9/2016 - 4/9/2016
Second Saturday at WAAAM Air & Auto Museum
1600 Air Museum Road
Hood River, OR

www.waaamuseum.org   541-308-1600

The Second Saturday of each month the WAAAM Air and Auto Museum opens the doors to roll out and run some of its antique airplanes and cars. Visitors watch airplane operations up close and may get to ride in old cars too. Open 9-5. Activities 10-2. Lunch 11-1. Free parking. WAAAM is located three miles from downtown Hood River at 1600 Air Museum Road, Hood River, OR 97031.

Paid Admission
Kid Friendly Event
Hours: Daily 9am-5pm

4/16/2016 - 4/17/16 (tentative)
NW Pet & Companion Fair
Portland Expo Center - Portland, OR
www.nwpetfair.com   (360) 281-3426

Paid Admission
Kid Friendly Event

Vendor Contact: lauren@nwpetfair.com

4/22/2016 - 4/24/2016
Northwest Cherry Festival
Downtown - The Dalles, OR
www.thedalleschamber.com/index.php/play/nort
hwest-cherry-festival   (541) 296-2231

Admission: Not Provided

Vendor Contact: info@thedalleschamber.com

4/23/2016 - 04/24/16 (tentative)
Oregon Ag Fest 2016
Oregon State Fairgrounds - Salem, OR
www.oragfest.com

Folks attend each year to touch, taste and experience
the incredible world of Oregon's agriculture industy.
Visitors come from all over the state to have fun and
learn about Oregon's largest industry. Children under 12
are free!

Paid Admission
Kid Friendly Event

Vendor Contact: info@oragfest.com
Attendance: 17000

4/2016 - TBA
22nd Annual Spring Beer & Wine Fest
Oregon Convention Center - Portland, OR
www.springbeerfest.com

Paid Admission
Vendor Contact: stevwoolard@aol.com

4/2016 - TBA
Blossom Craft Show
Hood River Fairgrounds - Odell, OR
(541) 354-2865

Admission: Not Provided
Vendor Contact: hrfair@hrecn.net
# of Vendors: 125

4/2016 - TBA
Cedar Hills Spring Artisan Bazaar
Cedar Hills Recreation Center - Portland, OR

Admission: Not Provided
Kid Friendly Event   Hours: 9am - 1pm
Vendor Contact: Bevin Bledsoe

4/2016 - TBA
Northwest Pet Fair 2016
Portland Expo Center - Portland, OR
www.nwpetfair.com   (360) 281-3426

Pet Food Drive, Pet Adoptions, Pet Costume & Fashion Show Contest, Doggie Relay Races, Marketplace, Yappy Hour Wine & Beer Tasting, live entertainment and more!

Free Admission
Kid Friendly Event

Vendor Contact: Lauren lauren@nwpetfair.com
# of Vendors: 75

4/2016 - TBA
YYFAP Talent Show
Yachats Commons Auditorium - Yachats, OR
(541) 547-4599

Everything from magic tricks to dancing, singing to juggling! Presented by Yachats Youth & Family Activities Program (YYFAP).

Admission: Not Provided
Kid Friendly Event
Hours: 2pm

# of Years Held: 15

May 2016

5/1/2016 - 5/3/2016
Cinco de Mayo
Waterfront Park - Portland, OR
www.cincodemayo.org

Paid Admission
Kid Friendly Event

5/14/2016 - 5/14/2016
Children's Nature Fair
Leach Botanical Garden, 6704 SE 122nd Ave.
Portland, OR
www.leachgarden.org   (503) 823-1671

Every year is a different nature theme that includes fun interactive activities for kids of all ages, families and adults.

Meet Audubon's education birds, explore interactive booths, create art & crafts, take a nature walk, enjoy music, 25 cent ice cream and more!

Partner's booths include: Audubon, Zenger Farm, Portland Parks EE program, Friends of Outdoor School, EEAO and Johnson Creek Watershed Council.

Admission: Free, Donations Appreciated
Kid Friendly Event
Hours: 10am - 2pm

5/14/2016 - 5/16/16 (tentative)
Pioneer Family Festival
Clackamette Park - Oregon City, OR
www.pioneerfamilyfestival.itgo.com

Teddy Bear Parade, Carnival, Food Court, Arts & Crafts
Vendors, Skate Competition; Scooter Competition, BMX
Competition, Rock Wall, Paint Ball Range, Pony Rides
and more!

Admission: Not Provided
Kid Friendly Event

Vendor Contact: info@pioneerfamilyfestival.com

5/14/2016 - 5/14/2016
**Second Saturday at WAAAM Air
& Auto Museum**
1600 Air Museum Road
Hood River, OR

www.waaamuseum.org   541-308-1600

The Second Saturday of each month the WAAAM Air and
Auto Museum opens the doors to roll out and run some
of its antique airplanes and cars.

Visitors watch airplane operations up close and may get
to ride in old cars too. Open 9-5. Activities 10-2. Lunch
11-1. Free parking.

WAAAM is located three miles from downtown Hood
River at 1600 Air Museum Road, Hood River, OR 97031.

Paid Admission
Kid Friendly Event
Hours: Daily 9am-5pm

5/14/2016 - 5/14/16 (tentative
St. Johns Bizaare Street Fair & Parade
St. Johns Neighborhood - North Portland
Portland, OR
www.stjohnsbizarre.com

Free Admission
Kid Friendly Event

# of Vendors: 50

5/27/2016 - 7/8/2016
Rose Festival 2016
Waterfront Park & Downtown
Portland, OR

www.rosefestival.org   (503) 227-2681

Beginning Memorial Day Weekend with CityFair, this
annual popular event is filled with parades galore,
Queen's Coronation, run/walks, golf tournament, rose
show, milk carton boat and other races, carnival rides,
plenty of live entertainment, exhibits, food and more!

Great fun for the entire family... an event that draws
people from all over the world!

Paid/Free Admission - Depending on Event
Kid Friendly Event

Vendor Contact: info@rosefestival.org
# of Years Held: 100

PORTLAND ROSE FESTIVAL

5/27/2016 - 6/10/2016
Rose Festival CityFair
Waterfront Park - Portland, OR

www.rosefestival.org   (503) 227-2681

Three weekends starting Memorial Day Weekend! Rose Festival overtakes Waterfront Park with rides, games, exhibits, Pepsi, food & entertainment in RoZone brought to you by KING 101.9 FM, The Bull 98.7 FM and Live 95.5 FM!

IFEA named CiyFair the Cleanest and Greenest festival in America, made possible by PGE and SOLVE. Proudly sponsored by Alaska Airlines. Season Passes available at Fred Meyer stores.

Paid Admission
Kid Friendly Event
Hours: See Website

Vendor Contact: Christie Wong info@rosefestival.org
# of Years Held: 100

5/28/2016 - 5/28/2016
Memorial Day Pie & Ice Cream Social
Yachats Ladies Clubhouse - W 3rd & Pontiac
Yachats, OR

This annual event is famous for the astouding variety of delicious pies! Come early for the best selection!

Admission: Not Provided
Kid Friendly Event

PGE / SOLVE

STARLIGHT
PARADE

5/28/2016 - 5/28/2016
Rose Festival PGE/Solve
Starlight Parade
Downtown Portland - Portland, OR
www.rosefestival.org
(503) 227-2681

This glittering illuminated night-time parade lights up the downtown! Come see for yourself the twinkling floats, drill teams & marching bands. The PGE/SOLVE Starlight Parade will also be aired live on FOX 12. Don't miss the Spirit of the West section presented by Spirit Mountain Casino and the special entry from Alaska Airlines!

Free Admission
Kid Friendly Event
Hours: 8:30pm - 11pm

Vendor Contact: info@rosefestival.org
# of Years Held: 100

05/2016 - TBA
BabyFest
Oregon Convention Center - Portland, OR
www.babyfestnw.com   (360) 514-0767

The Northwest's Biggest Baby Shower!

Paid Admission
Kid Friendly Event
Hours: VIP Entry - 10am;
            Show Hours: 11am-4pm

Vendor Contact: Lori lori@pintsizedproductions.com

June 2016

6/1/2016 - 6/1/2016
Fred Meyer Rose Festival
Junior Parade
Hollywood District - Portland, OR
www.rosefestival.org   (503) 227-2681

Thousands of children march through the Hollywood District in this parade just for kids! The Fred Meyer Junior Parade is televised live on FOX 12 Oregon.

Free Admission
Kid Friendly Event   Hours: 1pm - 2pm

Vendor Contact: info@rosefestival.org
# of Years Held: 100

6/4/2016 - 6/4/2016
Spirit Mountain
Grand Floral Parade

Memorial Coliseum to Downtown Portland - Portland, OR
www.rosefestival.org   (503) 227-2681

This cherished highlight of the Portland Rose Festival is a beloved tradition! Spectacular all-floral floats, bands & equistrians march through the Coliseum to downton. A Portland tradition! Watch the parade for free along the 4.2 mile route! The Spirit Mountain Casino Grand Floral Parade is proudly supported by Alaska Airlines.

Paid Admission
Kid Friendly Event   Hours: 10am - noon
Vendor Contact: info@rosefestival.org
# of Years Held: 100

6/11/2016 - 6/11/2016
Ceramic Mug Painting for Dad!
Spark Arts Center, 1805 NE Cesar Chavez Blvd
Portland, OR
www.sparkartscenter.com   (503) 281-6757

Paint a one of a kind gift for Dad that he will be truly
excited about! Choose from mugs, bowls, plates and
magnets.

Paid Admission
Kid Friendly Event
Hours: Saturday, June 11 10am - 2pm

6/11/2016 - 6/11/2016
**Second Saturday at WAAAM Air
& Auto Museum**
1600 Air Museum Road
Hood River, OR
www.waaamuseum.org   541-308-1600

The Second Saturday of each month the WAAAM Air and
Auto Museum opens the doors to roll out and run some
of its antique airplanes and cars.

Visitors watch airplane operations up close and may get
to ride in old cars too. Open 9-5. Activities 10-2. Lunch
11-1. Free parking. WAAAM is located three miles from
downtown Hood River at 1600 Air Museum Road, Hood
River, OR 97031.

Paid Admission
Kid Friendly Event
Hours: Daily 9am-5pm

6/11/2016 - 6/11/2016
Second Saturday at WAAAM Air & Auto Museum
1600 Air Museum Road
Hood River, OR

www.waaamuseum.org   541-308-1600

The Second Saturday of each month the WAAAM Air and Auto Museum opens the doors to roll out and run some of its antique airplanes and cars. Visitors watch airplane operations up close and may get to ride in old cars too. Open 9-5. Activities 10-2. Lunch 11-1. Free parking. WAAAM is located three miles from downtown Hood River at 1600 Air Museum Road, Hood River, OR 97031.

Paid Admission   Kid Friendly Event
Hours: Daily 9am-5pm

6/13/2016 - 6/13/2016
Cruisin' Sherwood Car Show
old town Sherwood - Sherwood, OR

www.sherwoodcruisin.com   503-625-2131

Cruisin is a great family event. Nearly 500 classic cars. We have over 50 of your favorite vendors with something for everyone. Food for every taste bud available. The kid zone has a whole park full of activities to keep the kids happy. Live music from local bands to keep you "hummin'" all day.

Free Admission
Kid Friendly Event
Hours: Sat June 13th 9am to 4pm

Vendor Contact: Roxanne tuprox@yahoo.com
Deadline: May 1st or when full
# of Vendors: 50+   Not a Juried Event
Attendance: average 15,000 – 20,000
# of Years Held: 25

6/17/2016 - 6/19/2016
Beachcomber Days
Through out the city of Waldport & Port of Alsea
Walpdort, OR
www.waldport-chamber.com   541-547-4173

"Come Live a Pirate's Life ™ at BEACHCOMBER DAYS 2016, celebrating our 60th year!

Friday: Port of Alsea, Captain Jack Sparrow, Jeff Curly Hair Magician, Music & Street Dancing! Lighted Boat Parade at Dusk & Pirate Costume Contest all ages.

Saturday: the Waldport Pancake Breakfast, Parade Hwy 101 & 34, China Restaurant Dragon Dancers, Vendors, Car Shows, Kid Zone, Camel Rides, Food, Music, Fire Dancers, Strolling Magic, Captain Jack Sparrow, Water Balls, Dress Like A Pirate & Treasure Chest Tickets.

Sunday: Port of Alsea Beach Sand Sculpting, Kite Flying, Keg Toss & Glass Float Hunt

Free Admission
Kid Friendly Event
Hours: Fri: 5pm - 10:30 pm;
           Sat: 8am - 10:30 pm;
           Sun: 10am - 2pm

Vendor Contact: Cheryl Stokes 541-563-4478
Attendance: 2,000- 3,000   # of Years Held: 59

If a June night could talk, it would probably boast that it invented romance.
~~Bern Williams, Philosopher 1929 – 2003

What is one to say about June, the time of perfect young summer, the fulfillment of the promise of the earlier months, and with as yet no sign to remind one that its fresh young beauty will ever fade.
~~ Gertrude Jekyll, British Writer 1843 – 1932

6/18/2016 - 6/18/2016
Blooms & Butterflies
Elkton Community Education Center
15850 Hwy 38 - Elkton, OR
www.elktonbutterflies.com
514 584-2692

A celebration of color in the gardens - includes a 5Kfun run along the Umpqua river, kids run, craft & vendor booths, BBQ lunch, gift shop, butterfly exhibit, native plant park, nursery sales, cafe, used book sale, information & demo biiths

Free Admission
Kid Friendly Event
Hours: Saturday 9-4pm

Vendor Contact: Joan Arsenault
info@elktonbutterflies.com
Deadline: 6/10/16
# of Vendors: 35   Not a Juried Event
Attendance: 300   # of Years Held: 11-12 years

6/24/2016 - 6/26/16 (tentative)
Festival of Balloons
Cook Park - Tigard, OR
www.tigardballoon.org   (503) 602-8213

Paid Admission
Kid Friendly Event
Hours: See schedule online

Daisy Photo by PDPhotos
All Free Download

6/24/2016 - 6/26/16 (tentative)
Lake Oswego Festival of the Arts
Lakewood Center of the Arts at George Rogers Park
Lake Oswego, OR
www.lakewood-center.org

Admission: Not Provided
Hours: See website schedule

Vendor Contact: center.info@lakewood-center.org
Juried Event

6/24/2016 - 6/26/2016
Lincoln City Summer Kite Festival
Beach at the D-River Wayside - Lincoln City, OR
(541) 996-1274

Kite flying demos, free kids kitemaking, and more! This
event has some of the most colorful big kites in the
world!

Free Admission
Kid Friendly Event
Hours: 10am - 4pm

Vendor Contact: events@lincolncity.org

6/24/2016 - 6/26/2016
Taste of Tacoma
Point Defiance Park - Tacoma, OR
www.tasteoftacoma.com   (253)759-8272

Free Admission (does not include zoo admission)
Hours: Fri & Sat: 11am - 9pm;
           Sun: 11am - 8pm

6/25/2016 - 6/26/2016
Nature & Art Festival
Rusk Ranch Nature Center,   27746 Redwood Hwy -
Cave Junction, OR
www.ruskranchnaturecenter.org   541-287-2164

The Nature & Art Festival celebrates the beauty and
bounty of our natural world and the rich art and cultural
resources of our region.

Arts, music, kids crafts, food, Wildlife Images, song,
Giant Puppets, Salmon Run Game, Pollinator Game,
Poetry Voices of the Earth, The Recycled Theatre Golden
Dragon play, Music, Food, Wildlife Images, Sustainable
Living Exhibit, and more!

Paid Admission
Kid Friendly Event
Hours: Sat June 25, 10-4
        Sun June 26, 11-4

Vendor Contact: Patty Downing
info@ruskranchnaturecenter.org
Deadline: June 1, 2016 (as space permits)
# of Vendors: 20-40   Juried Event
Attendance: 1500+   # of Years Held: 5

Green was the silence, wet was the light,
The month of June trembled like a butterfly...
~~Pablo Neruda, Nobel Price Winner for Literature in 1971,
1904 – 1973

It was June, and the world smelled of roses. The sunshine was
like powdered gold over the grassy hillside.
~~Maud Hart Lovelace, Betsy-Tacy and Tib Series, 1941
1892 – 1980

Mountains

Skiing

Kite Flying   Rock Climbing

Beaches   **Attractions**

Hiking

Waterfalls

Fishing

Sand Dunes

Whale Watching   Snowboarding

Horseback Riding

Camping

Surfing **Family Fun**

Bowling   Miniature Golf

Skating

River Rafting

Amusement Parks

AC Gilbert Discovery Museum
16 Marion St NE Salem OR
www.acgilbert.org

Paid Admission

Adventura
14300 NE 145th St Woodinville OR
(866) 981-8665
www.adventuraplay.com

Paid Admission

Adventura Center
40 N Main Ashland OR
(800) 444-2819
www.raftingtours.com

Admission: Not Provided

All Star Rafting
405 Deschutes Ave Maupin OR
(800) 909-7238
www.asrk.com/bend.html

The entire family will enjoy something water! Choose
from rafting, fishing or a kayaking adventure.

Admission: Not Provided

Alpenrose Dairy Tours
6149 SW Shattuck Rd Portland OR
(503) 244-1133
www.alpenrose.com

Your favorite dairy provides tours of the facility as well
as special events, such as Easter Egg Hunts, Midgit
Sprint Racing, and more!

Admission: Not Provided

Antique Powerland Museum
3995 NE Brooklake Rd NE Brooks OR
(503) 393-2424
www.antiquepowerland.com

Wed - Sun 9am - 5pm
Paid Admission

Aunt Bee's House
2679 Commercial St SE Salem OR
(503) 585-9749
www.auntbeeshouse.com
Hours vary depending on store. Please
see website.

This year-round artisan's mall is not your every day
vendor mall. From antiques to handmade creations,
seasonal décor to home décor, we've got it all and so
much more! Stop in to experience this hidden gem!
Three locatipms.

Free Admission

Belknap Hot Springs
McKenzie Bridge OR
(541) 822-3512
www.belknaphotsprings.com

Paid Admission

Black Butte Ranch
12930 Hawks Beard Bend OR
(866) 901-2961
www.blackbutteranch.com

Resort has horseback riding, biking, skiing, water sports,
fishing, and more outdoor fun for the entire family!

Paid Admission

Borden Beck Wildlife Preserve
Lower Bridge Rd Redmond OR
(541) 548-7275
www.raprd.org

Beautiful nature, hiking trails, fishing and swimming opportunities in the Deschutes River.

Admission: Not Provided

Bouncing Off the Wall
1134 SE Centennial Ct Bend OR
(541) 306-6587
www.bouncingoffthewallbend.com

Admission: Not Provided

Brice Creek Trail #1403
Umpqua National Forest - 25 miles southeast of Cottage Grove Culp Creek OR

Offers challenging terrain for intermediate and advanced bikers, hosting a 5.5 mile single-track trale and 5 miles of paved forest road.

Cascades Raptor Center
32275 Fox Hollow Rd Eugene OR
(541) 485-1320
www.eraptors.org
Nov 2015 - Mar 2016: Tues - Sun, 10am - 4pm; Apr 2016 - Oct 2016, 10am - 6pm.

On a wooded hillside in south Eugene come visit with hawks, owls eagles and more! Some 50 permanent resident birds are on display along gravel trails. Come get nose-to-beak with these magnificent Northwest birds.

Paid Admission

Children's Book Bank
1728 NE Glisan St Portland OR
www.childrensbookbank.org

Paid Admission

Chush Falls Trail
Forest Service Rd 680 Sisters OR

3 miles round trip. Provides viewpoint overlooking
Chush Falls. This is a nice trail for families who are
looking to get off the beaten path. Kids 3 & up will have
no problem hiking the trail unassisted and should wear
appropriate hiking gear.

Free Admission

Columbia River Maritime Museum
1792 Marine Dr Astoria OR
(503) 325-2323
www.crmm.org
Daily 9:30 am - 5pm

Paid Admission

Crater Lake
Crater Lake OR
(541) 594-3000

This is a MUST SEE lake. It has inspired visitors for
hundreds of years with its deep, pure blue color, sheer
surrounding cliffs, picturesque island and violent volcanic
past. Simply put it's a spectacular lake!

Admission: Not Provided

Deschutes Historic Museum
129 NW Idaho Ave Bend OR
(541) 389-1813
www.descuteshistory.org
Tuesday - Sunday, 10am - 4:30pm

Paid Admission

Discover Paragliding!
Warrenton OR
www.discoverparagliding.com

Paid Admission

Dune Bugs & Sand Boarding Fun!
68752 Hauser Depot Rd North Bend OR
9541) 660-5300
www.oregondunebugrentals.com/

Paid Admission

Eastern Oregon Fire Museum
102 Elm St La Grande OR
(541) 963-3123
www.unioncountychamber.org/pages/Museums

Paid Admission

Echo River Trips
116 Oak St Ste 1 Hood River OR
(800) 652-3246
www.echotrips.com/rogue

The Rogue River is the perfect river for beginners and families to experience river trips. The water is warm, the weather normally hot, wildlife abounds, and the rapids are exciting. Tour provides snacks, beverages, meals, transportation to and from the

Admission: Not Provided   Kid Friendly Event

Emigrant Lake & Waterslides
Emigrant Lake Rd Ashland OR
(541) 774-8183

The lake itself offers a host of family-friendly activities:
swimming, picnicking, hiking, boating, kayaking and
canoeing, fishing and tent & RV campgrounds. A 280-
foot waterslide is also in the park and open mid-June
thru Labor Day.

Admission: Not Provided

End of the Oregon Trail Interpretive & Visitor Info Center
1726 Washington St. Oregon City OR
(503) 657-9336
www.historicoregoncity.org
Sundays 10:30am-5pm Monday-Saturday 9:30am-5pm

The End of the Oregon Trail Interpretive & Visitor
Information Center offers hands-on educational
programs for all ages, the "Bound for Oregon" film, and
interactive exhibits on the trail journey experience and
life in Oregon Territory and Native American

Paid Admission

eNRG Kayaking
Multiple Locations Multiple Cities OR
(503) 772-1122
www.enrgkayaking.com

Paid Admission

Evergreen Aviation & Space Museum
500 NE Captain Michael King Smith Way McMinnville OR
www.evergreenmuseum.org

Admission: Not Provided

Flying M Ranch Horse Rides
23029 NW Flying M Rd Yamhill OR
(503) 662-3222
www.flying-m-ranch.com

Horseback riding as well as other outdoor recreational
activities. Children must be 7 or older to ride the
horses.

Admission: Not Provided

Fort Dalles Museum
500 W 15th St The Dalles OR
(541) 296-4547
www.fortdallesmusem.org
Open Spring - October, 7 days a week, 10am - 5pm.

A museum filled with historic wagons and antique
vehicles.

Admission: Not Provided

Frog Pond Farm
2995 SW Advance Rd Wilsonville OR
(503) 475-5997
www.facebook.com/thefrogpondfarm
Open for Christmas trees and Christmas cheer daily until
December 23rd, from 10 am - 5pm

Visit with the animals of the farm, shop the Alpaca store,
buy your Christmas tree, enjoy a cozy fire and hot
cocoa, cider or coffee.

Admission: Not Provided
Kid Friendly Event

Glowing Greens Blacklight Miniature Golf
Portland: 509 SW Taylor St
Beaverton: 3855 SW Murray Blvd
(503) 222-5554
www.glowinggreens.com
Sun - Thur 12pm-10pm; Fri-Sat 12pm - midnight

Portland and Beaverton's premier, black light, indoor, 18
hole, 3-D adventure miniature golf course. Stop in for a
great game of golf in our fun, memorable atmosphere.
We offer individual and group rounds for 18 or 9 holes of
miniature golf. Give your fam

Paid Admission

Helix Wheat Country
Helix area Helix OR

Bike trail surrounded by rolling hills of wheat fields and
majestic blue mountain view in the distance. Perfect for
the intermediate biker.

Admission: Not Provided

High Desert Museum
59800 S Hwy 97 Bend OR
(541) 382-4754
www.highdesertmuseum.org
May - Oct, 9am - 5pm daily

Explore your connection to the past, your role in the
present and all about the future.

Admission: Not Provided
Kid Friendly Event

Hood River Water Play
100 E Port Marina Dr Hood River OR
(541) 386-9463
www.hoodriverwaterplay.com

Many water activities await you and your family,
including: windsurfing, kiteboarding, sailing and more!

Admission: Not Provided

Hoodoo Mountain Resort
NFD 2690 Rd Sisters OR
(541) 822-3799
www.hoodoo.com

Plenty of outdoor activities for the whole family. Skiing,
tubing hill, snowboarding, snow-biking, cross country
skiing in the winter. Hiking and biking in the summer.

Admission: Not Provided

Howling Acres Wolf Santuary
555 Davidson Rd Grants Pass OR
(541) 846-8962
Closed Thanksgiving, Christmas and New Year's Day

Tours and special events provided. Howling Acres
provides a safe shelter for injured and orphaned wolves.

Admission: Not Provided
Kid Friendly Event

Inflatiable Kingdom
6830 SW Bonita Rd Tigard OR
(503) 718-0994
www.inflatablekingdom.com
Mon - Thur: 10 am - 6pm; Fri 10 am - 5 pm; Sat & Sun
9am - 1pm

Paid Admission

International museum of Carousel Art
Hood River OR
(541) 387-4622
www.carouselmuseum.com
Daily March 1 - October 31. Mar, Apr, May, Sept, Oct:
9am - 4pm; Jun, July, Aug: 9am - 5-pm

Free Admission

Jensen Arctic Museum
590 W Church Monmouth OR
(503) 838-8468
www.wou.edu
Visits must be scheduled.

Paid Admission

John Day Fossil Beds National Monument
32651 Hwy 19 Kimberly OR
(541) 987-2333
www.nps.gov/joda/

For the dinosaur lover in your family, take a trip to the
John Day Fossil Beds, which showcases fossils from the
Cenozoic era and the Age of Mammals. You may not see
dinousaur bones displayed, but you'll find an impressive
display of fossils from 65 mil

Admission: Not Provided

Jordan Schnitzer Family Art Adventures Summer Day
Camps & Teen Workshops
8245 SW Barnes Rd Portland OR
(503) 297-5544
www.ocac.edu

Paid Admission

Kid Time! Discovery Experience
106 N Central Ave Medford OR
(541) 772-9922
www.kid-time.org
Monday - Saturday: 10am - 5pm; Sunday: Noon - 5pm

Themed exhibits designed to stimulate learning through
hands-on imagaginative play. For kids up to 8.

Admission: Not Provided

Klamath County Museum
1451 Main St Klamath Falls OR
(541) 883-4208
www.museum.klamathcounty.org

Anthropology, History, Geology and Wildlife exhibits of
the Klamath Basin

Admission: Not Provided

Lake Oswego Hunt Riding Academy
2725 Iron Mountain Blvd Lake Oswego OR
(503) 636-1319
www.lakeoswegohunt.com

Paid Admission

Lan Su Chinese Garden
NW 3rd & Everett Portland OR
www.portlandchinesegarden.org
Daily, 10am - 6pm

Captivating architecture, peaceful environment, tea
room, gift shop and beautiful gardens make for a quiet
afternoon for your family!

Admission: Not Provided

Lava Lands Visitor Center
Hwy 97 at Lava Butte Bend OR
(541) 593-2421

If your kids are interested in volcanoes, this is a great stop!

Includes intrepretive trails: Lava Butte Trail, Trail of the Molten Land and Trail of the Whispering Pines.

Take plenty of water on hot days as there is little shade!

Free Admission

Lava River Cave
Hwy 97 S Bend OR
(541) 593-2421

Your family will have fun exploring one of the longest lava tubes in Oregon! Cave temperature is typically a typical 42 degrees, so wear warm clothing!

Free Admission

Learn to Surf
Seaside Surf Shop - 1116 S Roosevelt Seaside OR
(503) 436-1481
www.oregonsurfadventures.com
See website for Lessons & Camps Times

Paid Admission

Mad Science
1522 N Ainsworth St Portland OR
(503) 230-8040
www.portlandmadscience.org

Paid Admission

Malibu Raceway
9405 SW Cascade Ave Beaverton OR
www.maliburaceway.com

Let your kids enjoy themselves at this fun go-cart
raceway. Also has a few games inside.

Admission: Not Provided

Marine Park
355 WaNaPa St Cascade Locks OR
(541) 374-8619

A popular park offering camping, fishing, sailing and
riding the Columbia Gorge Sternwheeler. A playground
for kids and picnic tables available.

Admission: Not Provided

Medford Railroad Park
Berrydale Ave Medford OR
(541) 774-2400
www.southernoregonlivesteamers.com
Open to public April - October 11am - 3pm

Come ride the steamer trains! No cost to ride the trains
or look around the park. Park runs on donations.

Admission: Donations Welcome

Molalla Train Park
31803 S Shady Dell Rd Molalla OR
(503) 829-9124
www.pnls.org/
Open May - October, every Sunday.

All aboard! Park features miniature scale model trans,
trains - 5 steam, 1 electric, 2 diesel and 2 gas, and a 10
minute train ride, snack stand and gift shop

Admission: Not Provided

Mt. Bachelor Ski Resort
13000 SW Century Dr Bend OR
(800) 829-2442
www.mtbachelor.com

Dog sledding, skiing, snow boarding, snowshoeing and more

Admission: Not Provided

Mt. Hood Cultural Center & Museum
88900 E Hwy 26 Government Camp OR
(503) 272-3301
www.mthoodmuseum.org
Open 7 Days a Week, 9am - 5pm. Closed Thanksgiving & Christmas

Paid Admission

Mt. Hood Meadow Ski Resort
Mt. Hood Meadows Parkdale OR
(503) 337-2222
www.skihood.com

Fun for the entire family! Childcare for infants available 9am-4pm. Ski lessons for ages 3 - 6 also available.

Paid Admission

Mt. Hood Railroad
10 Railroad Ave Hood River OR
(800) 872-4661
www.mthoodrr.com

Offers the Odell Excursion Train (2 hours), Parkdale Excursions (4 hours), and features a Western Train Robbery Excursion train one weekend each month. Also the holiday Polar Express train and dinner trains.

Admission: Not Provided

Mt. Hood Ski Bowl
87000 E Hwy 26 Government Camp OR
(503) 272-3206
www.skibowl.com

Offers America's largest night ski area. Services include
skiing, snow tubing, snowboarding, kids super play zone,
private and group lessons.

Paid Admission

Multnomah Falls
Columbia River Gorge National Scenic Area
Bridal Veil OR
(503) 695-2372

Oregon's most famous water falls are a must-see! For
the hiking family, there is a system of trails that winds
between waterfalls along the scenic highway.

Free Admission

Museum at Warm Springs
2189 US 26 Madras OR
(541) 553-3331
www.museumatwarmsprings.org
Open daily, 9am - 5pm

This museum invites you to follow in the footsteps of the
three tribes who call the Warm Springs Reservation
home. This is a must stop place to see.

Admission: Not Provided

Noah's River Adventures
53 N Main St Ashland OR
(800) 858-2811
www.noahsrafting.com

Half-day and full-day Rogue River Rafting trips and 3-4
day adventures. Ages 8 & Up.

Admission: Not Provided

North Clackamas Aquatic Park
7300 SE Harmoney Rd Milwaukie OR
(503) 557-7873
www.ncprd.com/aquatic-park

This aquatic park offers a variety of swimming pools,
thee water slides, a wave pool, kiddie pool, hot tub,
fountains and a 29-foot rock climbing wall.

Paid Admission

North Mountain Park & Nature Center
620 N Mountain Ave Ashland OR
(541) 488-6606
Mon - Fri, 8:30am - 4:30pm

Home to an artistic spiral serpent sandbox, two
playgrounds, softball & baseball fields, soccer field and
concession buildings. The center sponsors three annual
events: Rogue Valley Earth Day, Bear Creek Festival and
Rogue Valley Bird Day. Discovery Kit

Admission: Not Provided
Kid Friendly Event

Oak's Park
7805 SE Oaks Park Way Portland OR
(503) 233-5777
www.oakspark.com
Varies - See Website

Roller Skating, Amusement Rides, Miniature Golf,
Carnival Games, Comcast Community Stage and Special
Events

Free Park Admission

Ocean Trails Riding Stables
370 N Vista Ter Pacific City OR
(541) 994-4849
www.facebook.com/pages/Ocean-Trails-Riding-
Stables/127359653984754

A must for all horse lovers in the family. There is
nothing like riding on the beautiful oceanside!

Admission: Not Provided

Old Aurora Colony Museum
15018 2nd St NE Aurora OR
(503) 678-5754
www.auroracolony.org

Kids will appreciate the frontier life demonstrations that
show the amount of work it took to survive day-to-day.
Museum houses five buildings, including an ox barn and
rough log cabin.

Admission: Not Provided

Operation Santa Claus
4355 W Hwy 126 Redmond OR
(541) 548-8910

The largest herd of domesticated reindeer in the U.S. is
here in Redmond! The Christmas-theme working park is
a fun place to see, with the reindeer traveling the nation
during Christmas time.

Admission: Not Provided

Oregon Air & Space Museum
90377 Boeing Dr Eugene OR
(541) 461-1101
www.oasm.info
Wed - Sun, noon - 4pm

Explore the world of wings 'n' space craft!

Admission: Not Provided

Oregon Children's Theatre
1939 NE Sandy Blvd Portland OR
(503) 228-9571
www.octc.org

Paid Admission
Kid Friendly Event

Oregon Coast Aquarium
2820 SE Ferry Slip Rd Newport OR
(541) 867-3474
www.aquarium.org
Summer: 9am-6pm daily; Winter: 10am-5pm daily

This is a great place to visit, with hands-on exhibits and
a fun way to learn about the coast's ecosystem.

Admission: Paid Admission

Oregon Islands National Wildlife Refuge
2127 SE Marine Science Dr Newport OR
(541) 867-4550

Spans more than 300 miles of the Oregon Coast.

Free Admission

Oregon Maritime Museum
SW Naito Parkway at Pine Near Waterfront Park
Portland OR
(503) 224-7724
www.oregonmaritimemuseum.org
Wed - Sat 11am - 4pm, Sun 12:30 - 4:30 pm

Paid Admission

Oregon Trail Interpretive Center
1726 Washington St Oregon City OR
(503) 657-9336
www.historicoregoncity.org
Daily 11 am - 4pm.
Closed Thanksgiving, Christmas and New Years

Paid Admission

Oregon Undersea Gardens
240 SW Bay Blvd Newport OR
www.marinesquare.com

Learn about the undersea life on the Oregon Coast.

Admission: Not Provided

Oregon Vortex & House of Mystery
4303 Sardine Creek Left Fork Rd Gold Hill OR
(541) 855-1543
www.oregonvortex.com

Paid Admission

Oregon Zoo
4001 SW Canyon Rd Portland OR
(503) 226-1561
www.oregonzoo.org
See Website Schedule

Paid Admission

Out 'n' About Treehouses
300 Page Creek Rd Cave Junction OR
(541) 592-2208
www.treehouses.com

If you and your family are looking for unusal
accommodations, then Out'n' About is for you!

A fantastic "treesort" that features treehouse
accommodations, swinging bridges, rope course, giant
zip, campfires and more.

Admission: Not Provided

Out of This World!
6255 SW Century Blvd Hillsboro OR
(503) 629-8700
www.outofthisworld.net
Daily, 10am - 9pm

Paid Admission

Park Lanes Family Entertainment Center
6360 SE Alexander St Hillsboro OR
(503) 641-2161
www.parklanes.net
See Website (depends on activities)

Free Admission

Pat's Acres Racing Complex
6255 S Arndt Rd Cany OR
(503) 266-7287
www.patsacres.com/
Varies depending on park's events. See website.

Children 8 - 11 are required to take a lesson for the
Go-Carts.

Admission: Not Provided

Pendleton Family Aquatic Center
1800 NW Carden Ave Pendleton OR
(541) 966-0212
www.pendletonparksandrec.com/aquatic-center
Open during summer vacation only

Three outdoor pools, several water slides, concession
stands, and shelter rentals.

Admission: Not Provided

Pine Mountain Observatory
State Hwy 20 E Bend OR
(541) 382-8331
www.pmo-sun.uoregon.edu
May – September

Learn what astronomers do and how they do it through
telescopes and digital CCD cameras. Guides will show
objects through the various telescoepes in the night sky.

Admission: Not Provided

Portland Aquarium
16323 SE McLoughlin Blvd Portland OR
(503) 303-4721
www.portlandaquarium.net

Open 365 Days, 10am - 8pm
Admission: Not Provided

Portland Art Museum
1219 SW Park Ave Portland OR
(503) 226-2811
www.portlandartmuseum.org
Tues - Wed, 10am-5pm; Thurs - Fri, 10am - 8pm, Sat - Sun, 10am - 5pm. Closed Mondays

This is the 7th oldest museum in the US and the Pacific Northwest.

Admission: Not Provided

Portland Rock Gym Kids Camps
21 NE 12th Ave Portland OR
(503) 232-8310
www.portlandrockgym.com

Paid Admission

Pump it Up!
9665 SW Allen Blvd Ste 110 Beaverton OR
(503) 644-3332
www.pumpitupparty.com/beaverton-or

Paid Admission

Putters Family Entertainment Center
1156 Hwy 99 N Eugene OR
(541) 688-8900
www.eugenesgamecentral.com

Miniature Golf, Laser Tag, Indoor Playground, Arcade, Billiards and, of course, Pizza!

Paid Admission

Ramona Falls Trail #797
65000 US 26 Welches OR
(503) 622-7674

This 4 1/2 mile loop leading to Ramona Falls is a popular
day hike. It's easy enough for young children. Come
see the beautiful falls that await you and your family!

Admission: Not Provided

Rice Museum of Rocks & Minerals
Hwy 26 at Helvetia Rd/Brookwood Exit Portland OR
(503) 647-2418
www.ricenorthwestmuseum.org
Wed - Fri: 1pm - 5pm; Sat & Sun: 10am - 5pm

Paid Admission

Richardson's Rock Ranch
6683 NE Haycreek Rd Madras OR
(541) 475-2680
www.richardsonrockranch.com

While it is a working cattle ranch, it is suplimented by
rock hound activities with its world famous agate beds,
featuruing thunder eggs and ledge agate material.
Some great digging fun for the family that collects
agates.

Admission: Not Provided

Riverside Greens Mini Golf
62102 Fruitdale Lane La Grande OR
(541) 963-7361
www.visiteasternoregon.com/entry/riverside-
greens-mini-golf/

Admission: Not Provided

Rogue River Hellgate Jetboat Excursions
966 SW 6th Ave Grants Pass OR
(541) 479-7204
www.hellgate.com
Daily. Some trips close for winter season.

Paid Admission

Rogue Valley ZipLine Advanture
9450 Old Stage Rd Central Point OR
(541) 821-9476
www.rvzipline.com/
Check days and times online as they vary due to the
time of year.

Nestled in the beautiful hills of Sourthern Oregon, there
are 5 zip line courses. Hoe of the longest zip line in the
Northwest. Riders must be at least 8 years old and
weigh between 70 - 270 pounds, in good physical
condition.

Admission: Not Provided

Safari Sam's
16160 SW Langer Dr Sherwood OR
(503) 925-8000
www.jungleoffun.com

Paid Admission

Salem Riverfront Carousel
101 Front St Salem OR
(503) 540-0374
www.salemcarousel.wix.com/salemcarousel

Free Admission

Sand Dunes Frontier
83960 Hwy 101 Florence OR
(541) 997-3544
www.sanddunesfrontier.com
9am - 6pm daily;
Winter Hours (Dec 15 - Mar 15): 10m - 4pm Tues - Sat

Single ATV rentals, guided sand rail tours, guided scenic
tours. Campsite or RV space located just minutes away!

Admission: Not Provided

Sauvie Island Stables
19430 NW Reeder Rd Portland OR
(503) 756-8904
www.sauvieislandstables.com

Paid Admission

SCIENCE Children's Museum & Exploration Dome **FACTORY**

Science Factory Children's
Museum & Exploration Dome
2300 Leo Harris Prkwy Eugene OR

(541) 682-7888

www.sciencefactory.org

Exhibit Hall Hours: Wed - Sun, 10am - 4pm;
Exploration Dome Hrs: Sat & Sun, 10:30 am - 3pm

Regularly changing exhibitions, planetarium programs,
birthday parties, special events, no-school day
workshops, holiday vacation & summer camps for kids

Paid Admission

Science Works Hands-on Museum
1500 E Main St Ashland OR
(541) 482-6767
www.scienceworksmuseum.org

Fall/Winter/Spring: Wed-Sun 10am - 5pm.
                        Closed most Federal Holidays.

Paid Admission

Sherwood Ice Arena
20407 SW Borchers Dr Sherwood OR
(503) 625-5757
www.sherwoodicearena.com

Paid Admission

Silver Falls State Park
20024 Silver Falls Hwy SE Sublimity OR
(503) 873-8681

Canyon Trail system that leads hikers along the north
and south forks of Silver Creek. Biking, skateboarding,
in-line skates and pets are not allowed on the trails.

Admission: Not Provided

Snow Bunny Snow Play Area
Government Camp Loop Government Camp OR
www.summitskiarea.com

A snow bunny snow play and tubing area for the little
ones!

Admission: Not Provided

Splash Lively Park Swim Center
6100 Thurston Rd Springfield OR
(541) 736-4244
www.willamalane.org/facility/splash-at-lively-park/

Offers swimming pools, water slide, wave pool, kiddie pool, fountains, hot tub and sun deck for those great sunny days!

Admission: Not Provided

Stoneworks Climbing Gym
6775 SW 111th Ave Beaverton OR
(503) 644-3517
www.belay.com

Hours: Mon/Wed 1pm-10pm;
                Tues/Thur 4pm - 10pm,
                Fri 1pm - 8pm;
                Sat & Sun 12-8pm

Paid Admission

Strike City Lanes
1156 Hwy 99N Eugene OR
(541) 688-8900
www.eugenesgamecentral.com

Bowling for the whole family! 24 lanes, video games, snack bar!

Paid Admission

Summit Snow Play Area
Government Camp Loop Government Camp OR
www.summitskiarea.com

Tubing fun for the entire family in an area that provides plenty of hills for downhill tubing fun!

Admission: Not Provided

Sun Country Tours
531 SW 13th St Bend OR
(800) 770-2161
www.suncountrytours.com

Something for the entire family in outdoor fun! Rent
tubes and enjoy a simple river float, or enjoy a river
rafting adventure!

Admission: Not Provided

Sun Mountain Fun Center
300 NE Bend River Mall Dr Bend OR
(541) 382-6161
www.sunmountainfun.com
Sun - Thur: 10am - 11pm; Fr & Sat: 10am - Midnight.
Some holidays have shorter hours.

Free Admission

Sykart Indoor Racing (Oregon)
7295 SW Hunziker St Tigard OR
(503) 684-5060
www.sykart.com
Mon - Sat: 11am-11pm; Sun 11am - 10pm

Paid Admission

Table Rock Hike
Table Rock Rd White City OR

Wear brimmed hats and take plenty of water on this
family hime. Upper Table Rock is slightly steeper, but a
shorter hike and the top is more fun! Filled with
wildflowers, lizards and other wildlife abound along the
trail. Kids will love flying balsa w

Admission: Not Provided

Tears of Joy Theatre
17 SE 8th Ave Portland OR
(503) 248-0557
www.tojt.org

Free Admission

The Dalles Talking Murals
404 W 2nd St The Dalles OR
(800) 255-3385
www.historicthedalles.org

Wonderful artwork that welcomes visitors and tourists
strolling the downtown area. Every mural features a
legened, which tells the story of an illustrated historic
event. Purchasing a key makes the murals talk by using
the key to activate the talking bo

Admission: Not Provided

The Great Cats World Park
27919 Redwood Hwy Cave Junction OR
(541) 592-2957
www.greatcatsworldpark.com
Daily, 11am - 4pm

This fun park is an interactive park where the staff and
trainers interact with the big cats. The cats at the park
have captivated audiences and features a varied
collection of exotic cats of more than 16 speciies.

Admission: Not Provided

The Oregon Garden
870 W Main St Silverton OR
(877) 674-2733
www.oregongarden.org
October - Aprii, Daily: 10am - 4pm; May - September,
Daily: 9am - 6pm

Paid Admission

The Village at Sunriver
17600 Center Dr Bend OR
(541) 593-5948

18-hole mini golf course, bouncy house area. A fun
place for the whole family

Admission: Not Provided

The Wax Works Living Museum
240 SW Bay Blvd Newport OR
www.marinesquare.com

Elaborate wax sculptures of famous people and
creatures.

Admission: Not Provided

Tillamook Cheese Factory
4175 Hwy 101 N Tillamook OR
(503) 815-1300
www.tillamookcheese.com
Mid June - Labor Day, Daily, 8am - 6pm

Get an up close look at how cheese is made and
packages, and, of course, FREE cheese samples!

Admission: Not Provided

Tillamook Naval Air Station Museum
6030 Hangar Rd Tillamook OR
(503) 842-1130
www.tillamookair.com
Daily, 9 - 5

What child doesn't love planes! Houses more than 30
war birds. Recommended for 6 & Up

Admission: Not Provided

Timerberline
27500 Timberline Hwy Government Camp OR
(503) 272-3311
www.timberlinelodge.com

Offers skiing year-round! Ski, ride, hike, snowshoe, and
camp all from Timberline!

Paid Admission

Tom McCall Nature Preserve
Old Columbia River Scenic Hwy The Dalles OR
(541) 298-1802
www.nature.org

The preserve hosts wildlife of every sort: horned and
meadow larks, wrens, red-winged blackbirds, a chorus of
frogs, mule deer and much more. Great Hiking to view
the bountiful spring wildflowers displaying their beautiful
colors.

Admission: Not Provided

Train Mountain Railroad Museum
36941 S Chiloquin Rd Chiloquin OR
www.trainmountain.org

Admission: Not Provided

Trillium Lake Trail
Trillium Lake Loop Rd Government Camp OR

Take a walk around Trillium Lake. In the summer, it is a
2 mile walk around the lake. In the winter, 3 - 4 mile
walk for snow sports. This is a wonderful, gentle hike
through the woods and long the shores of the lake. See
incredible unobstructed views

Admission: Not Provided

Troutdale Rail Depot Museum
473 E historic Columbia River Hwy Troutdale OR
(503) 667-8268
www.troutdalehistory.org

Featuring a wonderful collection of railroad tools and memorabilia exhibits.

Admission: Not Provided

Tubing & Adventure Park
87000 E Hwy 26 Government Camp OR
www.skibowl.com

Adventure Park is part of SkiBowl, allowing tubing for ages 3 and up, snowmobilling for ages 5 & up, snow bikes, and houses two stores of indoor fun for kids!

Admission: Not Provided

Tumalo State Park
Bend OR

Come float in the deschutes river and enjoy nature!

Admission: Not Provided

Upper Rogue River Trail
47201 Hwy 62 Prospect OR

Picture-perfect views. The lower trail is easier for kids. The river is accessible in several places, so be watchful of the kids!

Admission: Not Provided

West Coast Game Park
46915 US Hwy 101 Bandon OR
(541) 347-3106
www.westcoastgameparksafari.com
Oct 2015 - Nov 2015: Daily, 10am - 5pm; Closed
December. Jan 2016 - Sept 2016: See website hours
vary.

Paid Admission

White Wolf Sactuary
 Tidewater OR
(541) 528-3588
www.whitewolfsanctuary.com
Every Afternoon - By Appointment Only

Paid Admission

Wildlife Images Rehabilitation Center
11845 Lower River Rd Grants Pass OR
(541) 476-0222
www.wildlifeimages.org

Open for public tours throughout the year, featuring
birds of prey, mammals and reptiles.

Admission: Not Provided

Willamette River Bike Trail
Alton Baker Park - 632 Day Island Rd Eugene OR

6-mile bike trail that runs along the Willamette River

Admission: Not Provided

Wings & Waves Water Park
500 NE Capt. Michael King Smith Way McMinnville OR
(503) 434-4185
www.evergreenmuseum.org

Paid Admission

Wizard Falls Fish Hatchery
7500 Forest Service Rd 14 Camp Sherman OR
(541) 595-6611

A beautiful parklike setting, featuring display ponds. A
platform for viewing fish in the ponds is also available.
Best time to see the Canada gees goslings is May - June.

Admission: Not Provided

Yoga for Kids
1847 E Burnside Portland OR
(503) 893-5342
www.yogaforkidsportland.com
Studio Class Hours: Tuesday's, 4pm - 4:45pm

Features studio classes, birthday parties and yoga in
schools.

Paid Admission

*Whidbey Island
Garden
Photo by
Catherine Pittman
© 2012*

Become a Distributor of Our Guides!

*Applicable for the Print Version Only

Distributor Requirements:

♦ Minimum purchase of 24 guides at our wholesale price. Purchased at our website only: www.nwhappeningsguide.com
♦ Select Oregon or Washington Editions Only or Half & Half of Each Edition
♦ You set the price - we do offer a suggested price

Sell them at:
♦ Bookstores
♦ Farmers Markets
♦ Fairs & Festivals
♦ Craft Shows & Bazaars

Interested?

Contact Us!
Telephone: (503) 598-9861
Email: happeningsguide@gmail.com

Northwest Happenings Guide
a Subsidiary of
Pitter Patter Productions
Tualatin, Oregon

Alphabetical by City Event & Attractions

Albany

70th Annual St. Mary's Arts & Craft Bazaar

Albany Home and Remodel Show

Albany River Rhythms Concert Series

Christmas Storybook Land

Linn County Fair

Northwest Art & Air Festival

St Mary's Arts & Craft Bazaar

Town & Country Christmas Bazaar

Ashland

Adventure Center

Ashland 4th of July Celebration

Ashland Chamber Children's Halloween Celebration

Ashland Old Fashioned 4th of July

Emigrant Lake & Waterslides

Festival of Lights

Lithia Artisans Market

Noah's River Adventures

North Mountain Park & Nature Center

Science Works Hands-on Museum

Astoria

Astoria Sunday Market

Clatsop County Fair

Columbia River Maritime Museum

Talking Tombstones

Aumsville

Aumsville Corn Festival & Parade

Aurora

Old Aurora Colony Days

Old Aurora Colony Museum

Baker City

Baker County Fair

Christmas Trains

Fall Colors Train

Gold Rush Bandits Train Robberies

Grandparent's Day

Miners Jubilee

Parents' Day Celebration

Photographer's Weekend

Starlight Express

Bandon

West Coast Game Park

Banks

Oregon Garlic Festival

Beaverton

13th Door Haunted House

Beaverton High School Holiday Bazaar

Beaverton International Celebration

Malibu Raceway

Pump it Up!

Stoneworks Climbing Gym

Bend

Art in the High Desert

Balloons Over Bend Children's Festival

Bend Christmas Parade

Bend Fall Festival

Bend Summer Festival

Black Butte Ranch

Bouncing Off the Wall

Deschutes Dash Weekend Sports

Deschutes Historic Museum

High Desert Museum

High Desert River Outfitters

Kids Obstacle Challenge

Lava Lands Visitor Center

Lava River Cave

Mt. Bachelor Ski Resort

Munch & Music Series in Drake Park

Old Fashioned July 4th Celebration

Oregon High Desert Classic I

Bend

Oregon High Desert Classic II

Ouzel Outfitters

Pine Mountain Observatory

Shakespeare in the Park

Sun Country Tours

Sun Mountain Fun Center

Sunriver Nature Center & Observatory

The Little Woody Barrel Aged Brew & Whiskey Festival

The Village at Sunriver

Trail of Dreams Sled Dog Rides

Tumalo State Park

Between Gold Beach & Port Orford

The Prehistoric Gardens

Boardman

Boardman Thunder 4th of July Celebration

Boring

Celebration in Boring

Bridal Veil

Multnomah Falls

Brookings

American Music Festival

Brookings Harbor Community Bazaar

Festival of Art in Stout Park

Southern Oregon Kite Festival

Brooks

Antique Powerland Museum

Great Oregon Summer Steam Up

Brownsville

Bi-Mart Willamette Country Music Festival

Linn County Historical Museum

Burns

Harney County Fair, Rodeo, & Racemeet

Camp Sherman

Wizard Falls Fish Hatchery

Canby

Clackamas County Fair

Country Christmas 2015

Country Christmas Bazaar

Oregon Flock & Fiber Festival

Pat's Acres Racing Complex

Spring in the Country Bazaar

Canyonville

Canyonville Pioneer Days

Carlton

Carlton Crush Harvest Festival

Cascade Locks

Bonneville Fish Hatchery

Marine Park

Cave Junction

Haunted Candlelight Tours at the Oregon Caves

Nature & Art Festival

Oregon Caves Park

Out 'n' About Treehouses

Rusk Ranch Nature Center

The Great Cats World Park

Central Point

Christmas Showcase

Crater Rock Museum

Jackson County Fair

Rogue Valley ZipLine Adventure

Southern Oregon Holiday Market

Chiloquin

Klamath & Western Railroad

Train Mountain Railroad Museum

Condon

Gilliam County Fair

Coos Bay

29th Annual Holiday Lights at Shore Acres State Park

Bay Area Fun Festival

Coos Bay Wednesday Farmers Market

Mahaffy Ranch Pumpkin Patch

Corvallis

Benton County Fair & Rodeo

Corvallis Fall Festival

OSU Holiday Marketplace

Cottage Grove

WOE Heritage Fair

Crater Lake

Crater Lake

Culp Creek

Brice Creek Trail #1403

Depoe Bay

A Whale of Christmas in Depoe Bay

Indian Style Salmon Bake

Detroit Lake

Detroit Lake Street Festival

Elgin

Eagle Cap Excursion Train

Elkton

Blooms & Butterflies

ECEC Oktoberfest

Fort Umpqua Days

Enterprise

Hells Canyon Mule Days

Juniper Jam

Wallowa County Fair

Estacada

Estacada Summer Celebration

Estacada Timber Festival

Eugene

11th Good Earth Home, Garden & Living Show

33rd Lane County Home Improvement Show

37th Lane County Home & Garden Show

Art and the Vineyard Festival with Freedom Festival Fireworks

Cascade Health Festival of Trees

Cascades Raptor Center

Eugene Gem Faire

Eugene Saturday Market

Family Nature Discovery Days

Good Earth Home, Garden & Living Show

Lane County Fair

Museum of Natural & Cultural History

Oregon Air & Space Museum

Oregon Wedding Showcase

Putters Family Entertainment Center

Saturday Market's Holiday Market

Science Factory Children's Museum & Exploration Dome

Strike City Lanes

Westminster Holiday Bazaar

Willamette River Bike Trail

Florence

Florence Winter Folk Festival

Sand Dunes Frontier

Sandland Adventures

Sea Lion Caves

WFF Artisan Craft Fair

Forest Grove

Forest Grove Concours d'Elegance

Fossil

Wheeler County Fair

Garibaldi

Garibaldi Days

Garibaldi Days 2015

Gladstone

Follow the Star Living Nativity

Gleneden Beach

Gleneden Beach 4th of July Parade & Craft Fair

Gold Beach

Curry County Fair

Jerry's Rogue Jets

Gold Hill

Oregon Vortex & House of Mystery

Government Camp

Mt. Hood Adventure

Mt. Hood Cultural Center & Museum

Mt. Hood Ski Bowl

Snow Bunny Snow Play Area

Summit Snow Play Area

Timerberline

Trillium Lake Trail

Tubing & Adventure Park

Grants Pass

Howling Acres Wolf Sanctuary

Josephine County Christmas Bazaar

Josephine County Fair -- "Carnival Lights &
Country Nights"
Psychic Faire

Rogue River Hellgate Jetboat Excursions

Saturday Outdoor Growers' Market

Wildlife Images Rehabilitation Center

Gresham

Gresham Arts Festival

Haines

Haines Harvest Festival

Helix

Helix Wheat Country

Heppner

Morrow County Fair & Oregon Trail Pro Rodeo

Hermiston

Umatilla County Fair

Hillsboro

Affordable Art for Everyone

Brookwood Elementary 2016 Spring Bazaar

Every Husband's Nightmare Bazaar

Funky Junk Sisters Rebel Junk

Funky Junk Sisters: Rebel Junk

Oregon International Airshow

Out of This World!

Park Lanes Family Entertainment Center

Summer Festival

Washington County Fair

Hood River

Annual Hood River Fly-In

Blossom Time

Columbia River Gorge Quilt Show

Double Mountain Horse Ranch

Echo River Trips

Gorge Fruit & Craft Fair

Hood River County Fair

Hood River Holidays

Hood River Hops Fest

Hood River

Hood River Valley Harvest Fest

Hood River Water Play

International Model A Day at the WAAAM Air &
Auto Museum
International museum of Carousel Art

Last Chance Holiday Bazaar

Mt. Hood Railroad

Mt. Hood Railroad Christmas Tree Trail

Oneonta Falls

Second Saturday at WAAAM Air & Auto Museum

WAAAM Traffic Jam - A Car Show & Swap Meet

Independence

Western Days 2015

John Day

Keerin's Hall Holiday Bazaar

Joseph

Chief Joseph Days Ranch Rodeo

Oregon's Alpenfest

Wallowa Lake Go Karts

Kimberly

John Day Fossil Beds National Monument

Klamath Falls

Children's Museum of Klamath Falls

Favel Museum of Art & Indian Artifacts

Heart of the Basin Quilt Show

Klamath Falls

Klamath County Fair

Klamath County Museum

Klamath Falls Christmas Bazaar & Craft Fair

Quota Christmas Bazaar and Craft Fair

Saturday Farmers Market

La Grande

Eastern Oregon Fire Museum

Riverside Greens Mini Golf

Union County Fair

La Pine

La Pine Frontier Days

Lake Oswego

Lake Oswego Festival of the Arts

Lake Oswego Hunt Riding Academy

Lakeview

Lake County Fair

Lebanon

Crafters Market & Home-Based Business Expo

Old Car Sunday & BBQ

Seadog Nights & Gypsy Carnival

Lincoln City

11th Hour Santa Craft Sale

Celebration of Honor

Chalk Art Contest

Lincoln City

Hoops at the Beach

Lincoln City Summer Kite Festival

Taft Beach Sandcastle Contest

Wild Mushroom Cook-off

Lowell

Blackberry Jam Festival

Madras

Jefferson County Fair

Museum at Warm Springs

Richardson's Rock Ranch

Marylhurst

ArtBurst Northwest

Maupin

All Star Rafting

McKenzie Bridge

Belknap Hot Springs

McMinnville

Evergreen Aviation & Space Museum

Turkey Rama

Wings & Waves Water Park

Yamhill County Fair

Medford

Pear Blossom Street Fair

Holiday Bazaar at The Naz

Kid Time! Discovery Experience

Medford Railroad Park

Milton-Freewater

Muddy Frogwater Country Classic Festival

Milwaukie

North Clackamas Aquatic Park

Santa's Treasures Holiday Bazaar

Molalla

Molalla Train Park

Monmouth

Arctic Museum

Jensen Arctic Museum

Zimfest 2015

Moro

Sherman County Fair

Mount Angel

Mount Angel Oktoberfest

Multiple Cities

eNRG Kayaking

Oregon Truffle Festival

Myrtle Point

Coos County Fair

Newberg

Newberg Old Fashioned Festival

Newport

Lincoln County Fair

Mark O Hatfield Marine Science Center

Oregon Coast Aquarium

Oregon Islands National Wildlife Refuge

Oregon Undersea Gardens

Quilts by the Sea

Ripley's Believe It or Not!

The Wax Works Living Museum

North Bend

Dune Bugs & Sand Boarding Fun!

North Plains

Faerieworlds

North Plains 4th of July "A Wild West" Celebration

North Plains Elephant Garlic festival

North Powder

North Powder Huckleberry Festival "Huckleberry Fun!"

Odell

Blossom Craft Show

Ontario

Malheur County Fair

Oregon City

20th Oregon City Open Air Antique Fair

Christmas Fantasy Trail Wenzel Farm

End of the Oregon Trail Interpretive & Visitor Information Center

Halloween Fantasy Trail Wenzel Farm

Oregon City Open Air Antique Fair

Oregon Trail Interpretive Center

Oregon's First City Celebration

Pioneer Family Festival

Pacific City

Ocean Trails Riding Stables

Pacific City Artist Marketplace

Parkdale

Mt. Hood Meadow Ski Resort

Pendleton

Pendleton Family Aquatic Center

Pendleton Underground Tours

Philomath

Philomath Holiday Craft Fair

Portland

11th Annual Seafood & Wine Festival

22nd Annual Polish Festival

22nd Annual Spring Beer & Wine Fest

7th NW Annual Book Festival

A Christmas Carol

Portland

Alberta Street Fair

Alpenrose Dairy Tours

Alpenrose Easter Egg Hunt

America's Greatest Christmas Bazaar

American Indian Day Celebration

Art in the Pearl Fine Arts & Crafts Festival

BabyFest

Beach Blast Camp for Ages 5 1/2 - 10

Bite of Oregon

Cedar Hills Spring Artisan Bazaar

Ceramic Mug Painting for Dad!

Ceramic Ornament Painting

Children's Book Bank

Children's Nature Fair

Christmas Festival of the Lights

Christmas in Dairyville

Christmas Ship Parade - Columbia River

Christmas Ship Parade - Willamette River

Cinco de Mayo

Clay Studio for Ages 10-15

Concerts in the Park - Berrydale

Concerts in the Park - Columbia

Concerts in the Park - Couch

Concerts in the Park - Dawson

Concerts in the Park - Fernhill

Portland

Concerts in the Park - Glenhaven

Concerts in the Park - Kenton

Concerts in the Park - Lovejoy

Concerts in the Park – McCoy

Concerts in the Park - Mt Tabor

Concerts in the Park - Sellwood Neighborhood

Concerts in the Park - Ventura

Concerts in the Park - Willamette

Critter Camp for Ages 5 1/2 - 10

Curious Gallery 2016

David Douglas HS 18th Holiday Bazaar 2015

Division/Clinton Street Fair & Parade

Fashion Expo

Feast Portland Oregon Bounty Grand Tasting

Festa Italiana Portland

Flicks on the Bricks

Fred Meyer Rose Festival Junior Parade

FrightTown

G6 Airpark

Garden Home Recreation Center Holiday Bazaar

Glowing Greens Blacklight Miniature Golf

Green Festival

Hawthorne Holiday Stroll

Portland

Hawthorne Street Fair

Holiday Ale Festival

Holiday Bazaar

Holiday Marketplace 2015

Hoyt Arboretum

International Praise Fest

Jordan Schnitzer Family Art Adventures Summer
Day Camps & Teen Workshops
KidFest

Lan Su Chinese Garden

Laurelhurst Winter Bazaar

Leach Botanical Garden Holiday Bazaar &
Artist Market
Lents Street Fair

Lewis Elementary Holiday Bazaar 2015

Local 14 Women's Art Show & Sale

Macy's Parade / Holiday Christmas Tree Lighting
Mad Science

Mississippi Street Fair

Mississippi Street Fair 2015

Multnomah Day's Street Fair

Noon Tunes Summer Concert Series

North American Organic Brewers Festival

Northwest CiderFest

Northwest Food & Wine Festival

Portland

Northwest Pet Fair 2016

NW Pet & Companion Fair

Oak's Bottom Wildlife Refuge

Oak's Park

Oregon Berry Festival

Oregon Brewers Festival

Oregon Cash & Carry Gift Show

Oregon Children's Theatre

Oregon Maritime Museum

Oregon Museum of Science & Industry

Oregon Museum of Science & Industry (OMSI)

Oregon Zoo

Oregon Zoo Summer Day Camps

Oregon Zoo ZooLights

Paulaner Oktoberfest at Oaks Amusement Park

PDX Young Writers Camp for Kids Entering Grades 6 & 7

Peacock Lane Christmas Lights

Portland Aquarium

Portland Art Museum

Portland Artisan Market - Fall Market

Portland Artisan Market - Holiday Market

Portland Bead Faire

Portland Boat Show

Portland Children's Museum

Portland

Portland Christian Center's Holiday Gift Market 2015

Portland Christmas Cash & Carry Gift Show

Portland Craft Fair

Portland DeafNation Expo

Portland Expo Center Antique & Collectable Show

Portland Farmers Market at the Square

Portland Gem Faire

Portland Holiday Gem Faire

Portland Pancakes & Booze Art Show

Portland Pet Expo

Portland Reptile Expo

Portland Rock Gym Kids Camps

Portland Saturday Market 2015

Portland Saturday Market 2016

Portland Summer Antique & Collectible Show

Portland Vintage Racing Festival

Providence Festival of Trees - Portland

Quilt! Knit! Stitch!

Rice Museum of Rocks & Minerals

Riona's Cave of Treasures

Rose Festival 2016

Rose Festival CityFair

Rose Festival Starlight Parade

Portland

Run Like Hell!

Sauvie Island Stables

ScanFair 2015

Spark Arts Center

Spirit Mountain Grand Floral Parade

Spring Plant Sale

St. Johns Bizaare Street Fair & Parade

St. Patrick's Day 2016

Summer Concerts at the Zoo

Super Colossal Holiday Sale

Tears of Joy Theatre

The Blessing of the Animals

The Haunted Ghost Town

The Standard's 2015 Volunteer Expo

Tree Lighting Ceremony Presented by SmartPark

Tryon Creek Park

Weekend Guided Tours

Wilkes Holiday Bazaar

World Forestry Center

Yoga for Kids

Prineville

Crook County Fair

Crooked River Roundup Horse Races

Prospect

Upper Rogue River Trail

Redmond

All About the Horses

Borden Beck Wildlife Preserve

Deschutes County Fair & Rodeo

Home for the Holidays

Operation Santa Claus

Snowflake Boutique 2015

The Central Oregon Wild West Show

Rickreall

Polk County Fair

Rickreall Craft Festival

Riddle

Riddle Christmas Craft Fair

Rockaway Beach

Art Far & Farmers Market 2015

Fire Festival & Concert

Rockaway Beach July 4th Celebration

Roseburg

Douglas County Christmas Craft Fair

Douglas County Fair

Salem

AC Gilbert Discovery Museum

Aunt Bee's House

E.Z. Orchards Harvest Festival

Marion County Fair

Old Fashion Christmas in Salem

Oregon Ag Fest 2016

Oregon State Fair

Oregon State Salem Fall RV Show

Salem Art Fair & Festival

Salem Holiday Craft Bazaar

Salem Holiday Gift Market

Salem Home & Remodel Show

Salem Riverfront Carousel

Salem Wedding Showcase

Sandy

Rainbow Trout Farm

Sandy Main Street Fall First Friday

Sandy Mountain Fest

Sandy Oktoberfest

Sandy Summer First Friday

Seaside

Learn to Surf

Sandy Shores Gift Expo

Seaside Holiday Gift Fair & Parade

Wheels & Waves Car Show

Sherwood

Cruisin' Sherwood Car Show

Great Onion Festival

Robin Hood Festival of Sherwood

Sherwood

Safari Sam's

Sherwood Ice Arena

Silverton

Art in the Garden

Barn Dance

Christmas in the Garden

Fireworks in the Garden

Home School Day

Homer Davenport Community Festival

July 3rd Fireworks

Movies in the Garden

Silverton Fine Arts Festival

Stitches in Bloom Quilt Show

Sunsets in the Garden

The Oregon Garden

Sisters

Chush Falls Trail

Hoodoo Mountain Resort

Old Fashion Christmas in Redmond

Sisters Artist Marketplace

Sisters Arts & Crafts Festival

Sisters Fall Street Festival

Sisters Folk Festival

Sisters Harvest Faire

Sisters Wild West Show

Sixes

Cape Blanco Country Music Festival

Springfield

Oregon Whitewater Adventures

Splash Lively Park Swim Center

St. Helens

Columbia County Fair

Fall Festival & Pumpkin Patch

St. Paul

French Prairie Gardens Pumpkin Patch

St. Paul Rodeo & Wild West Art Show

Stayton

Santiam SummerFest 2015

Stayton SummerFest Car Show

Sublimity

Silver Falls State Park

Sublimity Car Show

Sunriver

Sunriver Art Faire

Sutherlin

Christmas Craft & Small Business Fair

Sweet Home

Sweet Home Arts & Crafts Festival

The Dalles

5th Annual Columbia Gorge Fiber Festival

Fort Dalles Museum

The Dalles

Main Street Summerfest

Northwest Cherry Festival

Starlight Parade

The Dalles Talking Murals

The Diamonds Bandstand Boogie

Tom McCall Nature Preserve

Tidewater

White Wolf Sanctuary

Tigard

Festival of Balloons

Inflatable Kingdom

Summer Lake Park

Sykart Indoor Racing (Oregon)

The Circuit Bouldering Gym

Tillamook

TCF Holiday Bazaar

Tillamook Art on the Green

Tillamook Cheese Factory

Tillamook County Fair

Tillamook County Pioneer Museum

Tillamook Naval Air Station Museum

Troutdale

Soulful Giving Blanket Concert

Troutdale Rail Depot Museum

Tualatin

ArtSplash Art Show and Sale

Autumn River Paddle

Family-Friendly Paddle

Kids Obstacle Challenge

River Clean-up at Tualatin Community Park

Sunset Paddle

Tualatin Crawfish Festival

Tualatin Farmers Market

West Coast Giant Pumpkin Regatta

Turner

Enchanted Forest

Tygh Valley

Wasco County Fair & Rodeo

Wasco County Fair

Veneta

Oregon Country Fair

Waldport

Beachcomber Days

Warrenton

Discover Paragliding!

Welches

Ramona Falls Trail #797

West Linn

Lighting of Maddax Woods

White City

Table Rock Hike

Wilsonville

Bullwinkle's Family Fun Center

Frog Pond Farm

Wilsonville Farmers Market

Winchester Bay

Dunefest

Winston

Wildlife Safari

Winston-Dillard Melon Festival

Woodburn

Wooden Shoe Pumpkin Fest

Wooden Shoe Tulip Festival

Woodinville

Adventura

Yachats

14th Annual Spring Craft Bazaar & Saturday Luncheon

46th Annual Original Yachats Arts & Crafts Fair

5th Annual Yachats Agate Festival

Annual Easter Egg Hunt

Crafts on the Coast Harvest & Holiday Arts & Crafts Festival

Memorial Day Pie & Ice Cream Social

Pathways to Transformation

Yachats

Spring Whale Watching Week

St. Valentine's Wedding Voe Renewal Ceremony

Yachats Lions Annual Crab Feed

YYFAP Talent Show

Yamhill

Flying M Ranch Horse Rides
